The Exquisiteness of Being Human

THE BODY, MIND, SPIRIT, SOUL DOMINANCE
THEORY

MARGOT McKINNON

A Spark the Spirit Productions Inc. Paperback

Dedication

For my mother, Audrey, who continues to inspire me...

For Elisa,

Here's to your Exquisite Experience.

Cheers!

Margot

CIP OpenInTeday
CRNied
InfraStruct
Prolu.

NERC

NAX

Electric
Riablity
CorpSSn
COP

FERC

Federal Energy Regul. Commissn.

Published by

Spark the Spirit Productions Inc.
In conjunction with Spirit Seekers Publishing, Inc.
Calgary, Alberta

This book is intended as a tool to explore the body, mind, spirit, soul, and God aspects of the human being. The theory was conceived of in a vision, and has not been validated through rigorous empirical testing. Therefore, the characteristics of each of the aspects and the suggestions outlined for each of the dominances may or may not be right for you. Every human being is unique. This book is not intended to replace professional medical advice. The publisher and the author expressly disclaim any responsibility for any loss or risk incurred as a consequence of the application of the contents of this book.

Cover design by Cecilia Humphrey
Photograph by Perry Thompson

ISBN 097800131-1

PRINTED AND BOUND IN CANADA

Acknowledgements

I will be forever thankful to Dr. Ian Winchester at the University of Calgary for designing a graduate level class on Spirituality and Education at a time when few were doing so. If he had not assigned the homework – "How are the body, mind, and spirit connected?" – I likely would never have had this most transformative vision. He encouraged me to share the message. 'Good teachers teach; great teachers inspire.' Dr. Winchester truly inspired me.

Soon after realizing the Body, Mind, Spirit, Soul Dominance Theory, I shared it with my high school students with the intent for them to poke holes in it and to determine if my vision was valid for the adolescent experience. The Body/Mind students found the theory quite logical, but were uncertain that the human being actually had a spirit living inside, a spirit that had distinct capabilities. Once these students cleared the classroom when the bell rang, the quiet, unassuming Spirit Dominant students hung around my desk. "Are you a mind reader?" some of them asked. "You just told me exactly what goes on in my head. I never knew why I feel so alone, and sometimes so sad," said another. Many of my Spirit Dominant students are failing school, designated Learning Disabled or Behavioral, or simply disengaged with life. I shared with these students that life is exquisite. To the students who found meaning in this new theory, who encouraged me to write my book and who checked in from time to time to make sure I wasn't slacking, I owe you all a huge thank you.

My own teen-age children Eric, Danielle and Alexander have been my motivation since the day they were born. I wanted to be the best mother that I could possibly be. But I am just a human being, one who can become grouchy at crunch time, one who burns the steak and gets the rice all stuck on the bottom of the pot, one who doesn't notice that the back step is falling off and that the paint is peeling around the doorframe and one who sometimes gets exhausted by the human experience and needs to retreat to my bedroom for a little afternoon nap. Thank goodness I have children who love me no matter what and who just laugh at my attempts at following a recipe or reading a map. Thank goodness I have children who realize that I have a purpose in life that is mine. Thank goodness I have children who encourage and inspire me to follow my path.

My father is another source of inspiration. He told me when I was growing up, "When you choose a career, choose one in which you are giving back to your community, one that is not all about earning a lot of money." He was right.

I need to acknowledge all those involved in the Sundance ceremony. They worked tirelessly and devotedly to re-establish this powerful healing tradition after the Sundance was declared illegal by those attempting to colonize and 'civilize' the Native Canadian people. Through the Sundance, the songs, the preparation Fasts and Sweat ceremonies, I learned to rise above my body and mind to strengthen my spirit, soul, and God aspects. I feel an enormous gratitude to all Sundancers and the Red Road that they follow.

To Sandra Delon, Wendy and Bob Fountain, Kathryn Christie, and Paul Day, thank you for making yourselves available to read my final, pre-edited draft and for making such wise comments. Thank you to Anna-Mae Sebastian, my editor, for believing in my work and giving me a discount because I am a single Mom trying to raise three children on a teacher's salary.

Thank you to my graphic designer and friend, Cecilia Humphrey, for her inspiration in designing the cover. She too believed in me and gave me a discount to help me reach my dream. I hope some day that I can repay her for her generosity of spirit.

Thank you to Michael Gelb, who read my manuscript on Monday and wrote an endorsement by Wednesday. I value his insights on human genius and hope that in writing this book I can convince others to recognize the early stages of genius. My desire is to participate in a change in how school systems view the human being so that Spirit and Soul Dominant individuals can have a better school experience.

Finally, I extend a huge thank you to all students, parents, friends and fellow researchers who support me in my journey to have Spirit and Soul Dominance recognized as a learning style in our education and medical organizations.

Table of Contents

Introduction

It's true; life really is generous to those who pursue their Personal Legend.[1]

Paulo Coelho (1947 -) in *The Alchemist*

ᔕ

Meet Santiago. In the book, *The Alchemist*, he was just a young boy when he set out to seek his Personal Legend. Along his journey, an old man told him, "People learn, early in their lives, what is their reason for being." He added bitterly, "Maybe that is why they give up on it early, too."[2]

Like Santiago, I learned early in my life that I had a Personal Legend, a purpose. But, unlike the bitter musings of the old man, I did not give up on it. My Personal Legend has been my driving force all my life. All decisions that I make are based on whether they will lead me closer to or farther away from my reason for being. Most people I know are still waiting to discover the meaning of their lives. I have known my purpose since I was four years old. It came to me by way of a mysterious voice beckoning me from some unknown dimension.

I vividly remember the first time I ever heard the voice. It came out of the blue. Every night before bed, while my family watched television in the basement, I would sneak up to the living room, dim the lights and say good night to my doll, Michael. In the corner was a tiny, wooden crib where I would place him gently after giving him a cuddle.

One particular night, just as I was pulling the blanket up around his shoulders, the silence was interrupted. "You are to be a teacher," boomed a deep, male voice. I knew that there was not another person in the room. I was alone. But I was not frightened at all.

"Okay," I answered, as I continued tucking my doll into his crib. No burst of light. No eerie figure standing beside me; just a deep, commanding voice with a sincere, straightforward, reasonable message. My purpose, my Personal Legend, was made known. I listened. I heeded. I have, to date, been a high school English teacher for twenty-three years.

How many people are given such a specific purpose to fulfill? How many people learn their message from a mysterious voice? Why did my purpose show up so early in my life and who was this voice? Was it my Guardian Angel? God? I wonder if I will ever know. Whatever the case, the voice was powerful enough that I am still teaching today. I have to continue on. I am compelled to, because I made a promise that evening when I was only a child.

Four years ago, for the third time in all my forty-six years, the voice returned. Each time this voice has spoken, it has added a new piece to the puzzle of my purpose. This time was no different. The deep, male voice revealed to me a theory about the nature of the human spirit. What I learned changed my life forever.

The voice challenged me to expand my definition of teacher. It urged me to stop taking my own spiritual encounters for granted and to start teaching others how to recognize their own spiritual gifts. The voice made me realize that many of us have forgotten how to relish the exquisiteness of being human.

From early childhood, I have known that there is more to being human than just having a mind and body. As a child, I regularly saw spirits, had visions and even roamed outside my body. I also had two near-death experiences, so I understood from a very early age that there is a spirit that lives inside me that is just like me, only intangible. When I die, my spirit will come out and go to a place of the most indescribable unconditional love. It will continue on.

This latest offering from the voice is the "Body, Mind, Spirit, Soul Dominance Theory". At the time, I was finishing off my Master's Degree and I was taking a course called *Philosophy of Mind*. Our professor posed the question, "How are the body, mind and spirit related?" as our first homework assignment.

To develop my response, I did what I have always done to get an answer to tough questions – I sent it out into the spiritual dimension and then waited for the reply. I was shocked at how quickly the voice from my childhood began to shape an answer. It has taken me four years to organize the vision that came in the form of words, complete thoughts and pictures.

Although the voice conveys through pure thoughts, it does so in flashes of insight. Clear messages, as though by mental telepathy, become fused with my consciousness. My struggle in writing a book was to find the words to describe the purity of the vision. I have refused to compromise the integrity of the vision by embellishing the stories, or using highly academic language as though to create more legitimacy about the ideas or by subtracting parts of the vision. Instead, I have attempted to keep the message as simple and accessible as the way it was related to me, so that anyone seeking answers to their own questions could read, understand and incorporate the ideas presented here.

If you are experiencing difficulties or challenges in your life, this book will hold some valuable answers for you, along with some unique strategies to improve your situation. If you have a child who continues to be an enigma, a mystery, this theory is for you. If your child has been angry and hostile since birth, the 'Dominance Theory' will open your eyes to the cause of his torment. If your marriage is breaking down and you feel numb and hopeless, wait for the epiphany. If someone you know has an addiction, you will suddenly look at that person differently. If you have a boss or partner that belittles you at every opportunity, this book will empower you.

Within the pages of this book, you have the opportunity to learn more about yourself, your partner, your children, your siblings, your colleagues and your neighbors. Ultimately, this book is not about changing who you are. It is about discovering more of who you already are and how you can strive to become more and more of who you are truly meant to be.

The question that I originally posed to the spiritual dimension was,

"So, how are the body, mind and spirit related?" I was lying on my couch, the lights were dim, a candle burned nearby.

Suddenly, I could see a force, like a light radiating outward. "There is a Force of Oneness," the voice said.

"Is this God?" I asked.

"Yes," the voice replied. It went on to explain that the Force of Oneness is planted in every human being, like a seed and, thereby, we are all related. From the Force, an infinite number of Soul Groups emerge. We all belong to a soul group in which we share a common purpose. Every human is issued a soul purpose, along with a spirit, a mind and a body to fulfill that divine purpose. Therefore, we are all made of five aspects that are overlaid and entwined.

As the vision unfolded, I was not surprised by the first part. Many writers have explored the five aspects of the human being. It was the second part of the vision that shocked me. It put my whole life into perspective and radically shifted my thinking of my relationships with others.

The voice revealed that each one of us is born dominant in one of the five aspects. We can be Body Dominant, Mind Dominant, Spirit Dominant, or Soul Dominant. It did not verify that we could be God Dominant, but suddenly, everything else made perfect sense. The vision revealed that there are people who thrive in their bodies who are physically fit and relish all of the sensual aspects of the tangible, earthly human experience. There are other people who are extremely intellectual, who prize their problem solving abilities more than they do their physical appearance or creature comforts. But the shocking part of the vision is that there are Spirit Dominant and Soul Dominant people.

I know that I have a Spirit Aspect that lives inside my body. It is more developed than my body and my mind. Yet few people think about what the capabilities of their spirit or soul are. If we know that our spirit will come out when we die, what is it doing while we are alive?

Our North American society has education and medical systems set up to serve the Body and Mind Dominant people. Yet, the vision revealed that there are many Spirit and Soul Dominant people who are suffering in silence because their needs are not being met. They are basically muzzled in the confines of our society.

We are comfortable with someone telling us that she talked to her father on the telephone last night, but not that she spoke to her deceased mother. We will accept an idea if there is empirical evidence, but not if it comes from 'intuition'. The 'way of knowing' of a Spirit Dominant person via intuition, the ability to see ghosts, have visions, or roam the spiritual plane is not exactly a prized skill in our society. It is in other countries, but in North America most spiritually gifted people keep their abilities a secret and try to function as 'normally' as they can in a Body/Mind Dominant society.

As a teacher, and as a parent, I see Spirit Dominant children every day struggling with the human experience. Sadly, quite often these children can be found in the learning disabilities or non-academic classes. They tend to have difficulties coping with school.

Soul Dominant individuals also struggle because they are the ones who are certain from a very young age that they have a divine purpose to fulfill. They are certain that all of their energy must be directed at this purpose even if it means separating from family members or living a life of solitude. Some will even die for their causes.

We are all very familiar with the person who understands that they have a body and a mind, but who scoffs at the idea of having a spirit. My vision showed me that there are people on Earth who are so Spirit Dominant that they do not realize that they have a body or mind. These people are autistic. The vision went on to show that several other developmental problems and mental illnesses can be understood better if we recognize that the individual is struggling with having been birthed onto the earthly plane and is in constant conflict with all that being here entails. We assume that every baby is born thrilled to be on Earth. However, many Spirit and Soul Dominant individuals find, to varying degrees, that having a body can be painful; that having to live within the confines of the body/mind reality is frustrating, if not downright intolerable. If anyone has ever had a newborn that shrieked and wrestled for hours on end, you know that your baby is resisting the human experience. If you had a child that spit out all new foods, could not accept change, had to wear the same shirt every day and/or would not participate in group activities, you know that this new theory is true. Not all children come to Earth willingly.

When I presented the Body, Mind, Spirit, Soul Dominance Theory to my high school class to get their opinion, I was shocked at the response. The Spirit Dominant students recognized themselves immediately. Typically, they were the invisible types in my class. They rarely submitted assignments and, basically, only attended in body, not in mind or spirit. When they saw the whole theory, they decided that they needed to become more grounded within their bodies and minds. They needed to find more pleasure in the human experience. I was shocked at how quickly they took to the theory and how instantly they wanted to make changes in their lives.

The theory changed my life too. I have spent far too many years retreating into my own spiritual adventures. Now that I am facilitating workshops on how to tap into the Spirit and Soul Aspects, I find that I must stay balanced by tapping into my Body Aspect. I am working on becoming more physically fit and on enjoying the dining experience more. I am learning how to enjoy the physical, tangible, sensual aspects of the human experience.

We can all learn that the exquisiteness of being human means to fully develop all aspects of ourselves – body, mind, spirit, soul and God.

I do not want to develop the whole theory here, but instead just give a glimpse into what you can expect from this fresh new perspective on spirituality. In Part One, I felt that a look at my own spiritual evolution was necessary in order for me to convey what I have learned about the capabilities of the human spirit. I have been studying what happens to my spirit when my body goes into trauma, how it responds to frustration and what it has learned through its own roaming. I give workshops now on the subject and consider myself like a fitness instructor, except I exercise the spirit rather than the body. This allows me to understand the Spirit Dominant people better, the ones who have a highly developed Spirit Aspect.

Because I know and understand that I have a body, mind and spirit, I study how all three respond to particular circumstances. My body has certain capabilities. For example, it plays tennis well, has a hard time stretching, prefers long distance running to sprints and becomes exhausted when I have too much to do at work. My mind also has certain attributes. It can concentrate for long periods of time, has a hard time calculating math and science problems, panics when it has to follow written instructions or follow a map and does not like to memorize. But how does my spirit respond to daily human life? How many people think about how their spirit is responding to stress or trauma? How many people are still unconscious of their Spirit Aspect?

Part Two outlines the essence of each of the five aspects: God, soul, spirit, mind, and body. This sets the framework for Part Three, which develops the idea that we are born dominant in one of the five aspects. For anyone interested in becoming a complete and whole human being, the vision suggests that no matter which dominance we are born with, we can fully expand and develop the other aspects in our human journey. I also include in this discussion the philosophical and scientific advances that have been made to prove the existence of spirit. Recent brain research and a genetic study presented in this section indicate compelling evidence that there is a 'God Spot' in the brain. Part Four explores more fully why some people do not enjoy the human experience.

I conclude this book with a call to action by those of us who recognize that our bureaucratic systems, especially in the education and medical fields, must recognize that the human being is more than just a body and mind. I urge parents and teachers to nurture children's natural spiritual understandings. I ask that medical practitioners take into account the spirit's role in illness and healing. Most of all, I encourage everyone to develop all five aspects of themselves so that they can be a thoroughly evolved human being, enjoying the exquisiteness of life.

PART ONE
My Spiritual Evolution

CHAPTER ONE

A Brief Look at My Story

But after that, she went on to warn me very seriously not to mention it to anyone else; other people, as far as she knew, did not have such pictures in their heads, either sleeping or waking, so it would be unwise to mention them.[3]

John Wyndham (1903 – 1969) in *The Chrysalids*

کہ

On the opening page of *The Chrysalids*, we meet David, a pre-adolescent boy who is confused about his vivid dreams of places and people that he has never seen before. He knows that somehow he is receiving a message from a far away land. His eldest sister, in her effort to shelter David from the suspicion and wrath of their community, warns David not to tell anyone of his dreams. "That was good advice, and luckily I had the sense to heed it," David decided.[4] He also knows that he has another gift that must be kept secret. He and several other children have mental telepathy. Their biggest fear is that some day their society will find out.

Nobody told me to keep my spiritual encounters a secret. In fact, until I was sixteen years old, I thought everybody developed their knowledge from visions, ghosts and out of body travels. As I grew older, I tracked my spiritual encounters so that I could learn how adventurous my spirit actually was. Unlike David, I do not keep my gifts a secret. I will tell anyone about my spiritual experiences, despite the warnings that I have received from family and professors worried about my academic reputation.

As I venture out on the journey of teaching the Dominance Theory, I feel that I must reveal my own spiritual evolution. By doing so, I can share my own personal struggle with being acutely aware of my Spirit Aspect while living in a society that does not particularly value spiritual wisdom. I also hope to convey the idea that the human spirit is incredibly active and powerful.

Childhood

Ever since I was a four-year-old, I knew that there were two realities. I knew there was an exciting, colorful reality that I could immerse my body in and explore through my five senses. But, I also knew that I was a spirit that had taken on the human form and had to fulfill a specific purpose. I was sent to Earth for a reason and I knew it.

In my first reality, I grew up as most other little girls did. I had a lot of friends and I played the typical childhood games with them, roaming the neighborhood on bicycles, spending hours at the local playground wrestling on the monkey bars, playing baseball, or setting up my favorite game of hide and go seek. I made prank phone calls to whomever I was in love with that week, egged on by my friends giggling in the background. I enjoyed coming home from school, opening up the front door to the smell of a stew on the stove, spaghetti sauce bubbling, or even the smell of fresh wax on the hardwood floors.

What was not so typical, although I never understood that at the time, was that I knew there was another reality overlaying the one in which I played with my friends, loved my family and worked hard at school. There was a reality that connected me to another dimension, a spiritual one that held truths that were mostly inaccessible through the five senses. There was a guiding force that let me know things that others did not.

I took my commitment of becoming a teacher very seriously – only wavering once. As a university student, I had a very cool job as a bartender around the swimming pool of a large chain hotel. The manager wanted me to enroll in the management training program, as apparently the pool bar had been a losing venture until I took it over. I toyed with the idea over the summer, imagining myself working all over the world and meeting with fascinating people. Ultimately, I could not accept the offer because deep down I knew that I was put on Earth with the expectation that I was to be a teacher. I could not break my promise.

That one significant message was not my only encounter with the spiritual dimension. As a child, I regularly saw spirits, especially at night in my bedroom and at my grandmother's house. Sometimes rooms were filled with spirits, as though a cocktail party were in full swing. I knew that even though the people I saw were not flesh and blood, to me they were still 'real'.

On occasion, I would tell my grandmother about the lady that I saw on the stairway, or the people standing in the doorway of a bedroom in her home and she would say, "Oh, they are always here." That was that. She saw them, too. I came away thinking that everyone could see spirits. It was a normal, everyday experience. These spirits did not have any particular message for me. To this day, I am not sure why I saw them.

My strength seemed to be that I had a profound sense of 'knowingness'. Around the age of ten, I had a very significant vision. Again, I was in my living room. Out of the blue, I heard: "die, 36, breast cancer, you will miss your Mom." Up until I was thirty-six years old, I thought that I was going to die of breast cancer. As it turned out, my mother died of breast cancer when I was thirty-six.

This vision and the visitations of spirits at night often frightened me, but I believed at the time that this was normal for all people, so I did not make too much of it. As a young girl, I was disturbed to see strange faces peering at me through the darkness of the night. I felt as though I was being watched all of the time. Only a few years ago, my older sister revealed to me that I used to frighten her when I was a child because I would crawl into the bed that we shared and comment, "How are we supposed to sleep with all of these people in the hallway?" She only saw a dimly lit space, while I saw several people laughing and chatting outside our doorway. She told me that she used to pull the blanket up over her head, spooked by what I saw.

The visions were not always frightening. I was also aware that the spiritual reality was a peaceful, loving one. And I had a deep longing to embrace that reality. It seemed so much better than the harsh reality of the tangible world. In it, I was completely free. At times, I would lie on my bed, breathing in and out, and think, "This is so hard, to do this all day." Breathing, for me, was labor intensive. I had an innate understanding that I was lugging around this body and that it was so heavy and limited in what it could do. I needed space every day to escape from the hustle and bustle of life, just to lie on my bed and let my spirit soar to places that it wanted to visit.

I felt as if I always knew that I had at least two selves, one body and one spirit. My spirit lived inside my body and it looked out through my eyes. Often, I would have the sensation of looking at my body and wondering, "Am I really here in body or is this an experience of spirit?" I also had the sensation that my spirit was not always where my body was. Sometimes my body, because of family or other human obligations, had to go places that my spirit did not feel like going; places like school, or to a party, or some other activity. I constantly felt, "Is this over yet? Can I go home now?"

But this encroaching feeling went even further, when on a couple of occasions, I pulled out the butcher knife in our kitchen and pressed it up against my seven year old chest, deciding that I had had enough of the human experience and wanted to go 'home'. Perhaps I should have excluded this particular longing, but in all fairness to my vision, I cannot. Perhaps one of you, or someone you know, has had the same feelings. Obviously, I did not do it, but the sensation of being exhausted by the human experience was at times, and on occasion still is, overwhelming.

To be at peace, I need a lot of quiet time to myself, or else I become quite irritated. I call it 'white space' time. All in all, I was well aware that I walked in two worlds at once, a physical earthly one and an ethereal spiritual one.

The Teen Years

Up until I was sixteen years old, I thought that everyone heard voices, saw spirits and had visions. By then, the 'knowingness' grew to the point where I picked up information that helped me in my everyday life, like roads to avoid while driving, or items that I needed to bring, just in case. It even got to the point where if I picked up a person's glove that was dropped on the ground, a flash of the person's deepest fear or deepest longing came across my mind. I felt like an intruder in other people's lives.

At sixteen, I also received visits from the spirit of my paternal grandfather three or four times a week. He died a month before I was born, but I always felt close to him. Each visit started in approximately the same way. I got the sense that he was going to make an appearance and so I would clean up my extremely untidy teen-age bedroom, and leave my door slightly ajar so that he knew he was invited in. When my grandfather appeared, he would walk through the opening in the doorway and sit on the edge of my bed. We spoke in pure thought, mental telepathy. Usually, he just asked about my day, the usual grandfather conversation.

At that time, I was taking a psychology class at school, and the theme soon turned to the concept of schizophrenia. I learned that patients who suffered from this mental illness claimed to hear voices in their heads, had visions and talked to people who really were not there. Naturally, I became nervous that I was actually mentally ill and not spiritually in tune, after all.

I revealed to my younger sister that I was receiving visits from our grandfather. She and I are only a year apart in age and were raised like twins. It was not surprising to me to find out that our paternal grandmother was visiting her. She had thought that it was all her imagination, until I told her about my visits. We decided to ask our grandparents what they wanted from us. We both received the same message – that our father need no longer worry or wonder what had happened to them after they died. My grandmother had died a few years before my grandfather, but they had reunited in the afterlife and they now traveled together.

One day, my sister and I decided to relate the message to our father, after we were sure that these visits were not just figments of our imagination. Being a scientist, he did not believe us at first. We decided to ask our grandparents to give us signs that only our father would understand. My sister would smell lilac, even in the middle of winter. That was our grandmother's favorite scent. When my sister wrote her midterm exams, each exam came back with the same date written at the top of the page... my grandmother's birthday. Our father rarely talked about his parents to us. We had never met them and certainly did not know when their birthdays were. When my father finally did believe there was something to our stories, I saw my grandfather standing there in our living room. He smiled and disappeared and I have not seen him since.

At this time, I still was under the impression that everyone saw spirits and had visions. One day, I found out for sure that not everybody saw the two realities that I did. I was sitting in my grade eleven English class, listening to my teacher emphasize to us that, in a particular story we were studying, the people of the time were uneducated and were, therefore, very superstitious. They believed in ghosts and premonitions. Although I was generally a very shy student, rarely raising my hand to volunteer an answer, I was compelled, on this occasion, to challenge the teacher. "What do you mean the people were uneducated and believed in ghosts? Ghosts are real. Can't you see them?"

At that moment, I finally found out that not all people could see what I saw. And it was that day that planted the seed for my desire; the desire to understand why some people can hook into a spiritual reality and why some cannot; the desire to understand why I was given this 'way of knowing' and what I was supposed to use it for. I refused to discount my experiences. They were real to me and affected me more profoundly than any of my more tangible, everyday experiences, like going to school, or playing sports.

In my first year of university, at eighteen years of age, I found out that my spirit could indeed separate from the prison of my body; that it could come out and have its own experiences. I discovered that my spirit looked just like me, tall with light brown hair and brown eyes – my twin, only intangible. This separation of spirit from body occurred a few months into my first term, when I spiked a very high fever. The university physician placed me in the infirmary of my dormitory, which happened to be in the basement. A student nurse was monitoring my situation, hoping to reduce my fever enough to send me home.

The nurse sat at my bedside and we gabbed away about what most young women usually talk about – guys. She finally got around to telling me that she had her eye on this guy for so long and he had finally asked her out for that Friday night. She could not go because she was assigned to look after me. Well, what could I say to that? I told her to go on the date; that I would be okay. She promised to telephone a few times in the evening to check on me. Excited and grateful, she left. Meanwhile, I fell asleep and had a dream.

I dreamed I was on the ceiling of the infirmary, flying toward a magnificent, glorious, orange light. Filled with passion, I was euphoric at the absolute freedom I felt as I was propelled toward the bright, orange ball of light. Suddenly, I was overcome with an urgent desire to say good-bye to my roommate and dear friend, Sue.

Still on the ceiling, I flew out of the basement infirmary. At the top of the stairs, in the front lobby of the dormitory, I looked down at several girls dressed in evening gowns, waiting for taxis. I paused for a second or two to look at them. One girl looked up at me, startled. We locked eyes. Somewhat of a tease, I did a somersault in the air and said, "You have seen your first ghost!" Then I took off to the fourth floor. I zipped through the door, looked down, no Sue. "I have to go," I thought and sped back out toward the orange light, feeling excited and free. Then I woke up.

Soon after, the nurse came rushing into my room. "I phoned you at nine o'clock and let the phone ring thirty six times. I thought you were dead."

"I think I was," I answered. "Were the girls going somewhere tonight?"

"Yes, some of them were going to the military college for a dinner dance."

"I saw them."

"How could you?" she questioned. "You can't even get out of bed."

When I was well again, I searched for the girl who looked up at me, but I never did see her again.

After that near death experience, or dream, I fully understood that we all have at least two selves – a physical, tangible body with the capability to eat, drink, walk, etc., as well as a spirit self that has capabilities of its own.

I developed an insatiable desire to understand my Spirit Aspect, to discover the full range of spirit capabilities.

If my Spirit Aspect is present at death, then what is it doing while I am alive? I have made it my life's mission to distinguish between my Mind Aspect and my Spirit Aspect. Just as an Olympic athlete wants to know how far he or she can push the body to reach its maximum potential, or a neuroscientist desires to know the full capability of the human brain, I am compelled to realize the full range of the human spirit.

Adulthood

In my twenties I lived in Beijing, China for a year, while teaching English with my husband, David. During our winter holiday, we traveled to the remote hill tribes of Thailand. The scenery of the jungle was vibrant and out of the realm of my human experience, especially when seen from the back of an elephant. The food had flavors that I still cannot even describe. In fact, if you were to ask me what my favorite meal of my lifetime was, I would have to say the seafood curry I was served in a bamboo hut restaurant, the ocean lapping up to our table.

Although we went to Thailand for an outrageous, sensual experience, I ended up getting so much more. I came away from Thailand a changed person.

The monks in Thailand are revered. They are ever present in the streets and in the temples. Most families have at least one member inducted into a monastery. Honoring the spirit was a way of life. Outside most homes stood a spirit house. It looked like a birdhouse, but the inside was adorned with food, candles and other offerings. The belief was that everyone needed to honor the spirit of those who passed over. What the Thai people have always understood is that the spirits of those who passed over know to go to the spirit house, rather than the main house. Even fire stations, police departments and hospitals had spirit houses out front. I had gone for a few years thinking that I was abnormal for seeing spirits and having premonitions. In my mid twenties, I discovered there was a whole country outwardly honoring the Spirit Aspect of the human being.

One evening, as we rested in one of the hill tribes, our guide began to tell us some stories about the people. The part that struck me most was when he said, "There are two kinds of people in the world – those who still have their spiritual knowledge and those who have lost it." He went on to explain that in the hill tribes, the people must nurture and develop their Spirit Aspect in order to survive. For them, it is a survival skill. If a woman wanted to talk to her mother who lived three hills over, she had two choices. She could either trek through the dangerous jungle, or she could use her mental telepathy. Our guide believed that many westerners have allowed their Spirit Aspect to wither away because we rely so heavily on technology to pass our messages along. If we want to talk to our mother, we can just pick up the telephone. We no longer need to keep our intuition and telepathic powers strong and alert.

While I was traveling, access to the telephone and mail service was very limited. I missed my sister, Anne, terribly. To combat this feeling, I used to sit in my chair and imagine that I would visit her. Because of the time difference, she was either sleeping or at work whenever I would show up in spirit. I zipped around the ceiling of her apartment, looked around and then with a blast of energy, I would return to my body. What a surprise it was to receive a letter from her, saying that whenever my name was mentioned in her apartment, something glass would break – a vase, a light fixture, a glass pan. I promised to stop visiting and she did not have anything else broken.

My husband, David, even came back from a camping trip to the Great Wall of China with a story of his own. While he was on his trip, I was traveling with my girlfriends. Bedtime came. I decided to send my spirit to him to say good night. When David returned, he revealed that he had the shock of his life when I appeared in his sleeping bag to say good night. He could not believe how this was possible. That was normal to me, but not to him. Our tour guide was right. My ability to pick up messages from the universe and send my spirit on missions is heightened when I cannot rely on technology to send the message for me.

During our summer holiday that year, David and I went on a pilgrimage through Tibet. Again, we did not really have any expectations, except that we knew we were embarking on an adventure that few had ever had. We joined in with the pilgrims and trekked to the temples in and around Lhasa, the holy city. We bought prayer beads, spun the prayer wheels, prostrated from temple to temple and learned the chant. Again, I was amazed that the Spirit Aspect of the human being was celebrated in such an outward, tangible way. Most people in our culture keep their spiritual experiences secret for fear of appearing a flake, or uneducated. In Tibetan society, the spiritual quest was the norm.

One particularly thrilling experience that I had while in Lhasa occurred when a monk approached David and I and told us to visit a special ceremony at a particular temple. We went straight over and stood at the back of the open-ended temple, peering over the shoulders of countless Tibetan pilgrims and the token sprinkling of Westerners. Suddenly, an elderly monk appeared at my side and beckoned me to move through the crowd to the front of the temple. He motioned for me to sit down with all of the elderly monks and to pray with them. Did he see my deep desire to understand the Spirit Aspect of the human being? To this day, I still contemplate the full meaning behind that exquisite moment in time.

By the time I reached my thirties, I was back in Canada, raising children. Unfortunately, I ended up divorcing my husband. Sad and disillusioned, I persevered with understanding my spirit, as it dealt with the most critical time of my life. The emotional upheaval of my divorce tested my body, my mind and my spirit. To make matters worse, my mother was suffering from breast cancer. She was always happy and good-natured, a hilarious woman, who often turned her misery into a very funny story.

I loved my mother and constantly felt that living on the other side of the country prevented me from helping her cope with her illness. To make myself feel better, I would let my spirit travel to her and clean her cancer away. I would visualize her organs from top to bottom and, in a sweeping movement, clean all the cancer cells out of her brain, heart and organs. Then I would start at the crown of her head and start again, cleaning out the cancer through the soft tissue, especially her breasts. Once finished, I would start again at her crown and clean her bones, then her blood, then skin, then spirit.

The very first time I conducted this 'cancer cleansing' my mother telephoned me and asked if I had been to visit her. I asked her to explain what she saw. She told me that she felt as though someone were cleaning her out with a paintbrush, in a sweeping motion and when she looked up, I was standing by her bed. Never, in my wildest imagination did I realize that my visualization would actually allow her to see my spirit standing by her bedside. When she received her report from the doctor, she was given a clean bill of health. Unfortunately, I revealed the story to a few close friends and was mocked for believing that I had anything to do with my mother's survival. How could I possibly believe that, by imagining my mother, way off on the other side of the country, I would be able to do any sort of cleansing? According to them, I was untrained and incapable. I stopped doing the spiritual cleanses. My mother died. At that time, I was not far enough along in my spiritual evolution to understand that what they said was not true.

Living in Alberta, Canada, I was fortunate enough to be exposed, repeatedly, to the Native Canadian healing practices. I participated in four Native Canadian Sundances. This ceremony is an opportunity to test the body, mind and spirit because it is a rigorous test of endurance. I knew that our Spirit Aspect is powerful beyond our understanding. I was sure that the fasting, dancing and piercing in the hot sun would show me how far I could push my Spirit Aspect. My second Sundance led to my second near-death experience.

I had just returned to the circle after being pierced on both arms. The sun beat down upon our heads. I had not eaten in three days and I could not stand the sight of blood from the piercing. Everything started to spin and turn white. The next thing I knew, I was flat on my back, moving up to a space of pure whiteness. My mother, who had recently passed over, was smiling at me with her trademark wide grin. The whiteness I saw was not a place, but a euphoric feeling of the most brilliant, unconditional love imaginable, just like my mother's smile. I was excited and euphoric, just as I was in my first near death experience. My body, mind and spirit became fused with this unconditional love. In fact, I had to open my eyes as big as I could get them, which meant that I had to open my mouth wide, to allow my eyes to be wider. I felt as if I were drinking in the unconditional love; that it and I were one.

My mother looked at me and said, "You can't come with me. It is not your time." Suddenly, I heard my friend urgently calling my name and my spirit was sucked back into my body. My eyes were still huge and my mouth was still open wide. A year earlier, I was blessed to be with my mother when she passed. Her eyes were huge and her mouth was wide open. Now I know what she was looking at when she passed. She was going into the most magnificent, unconditional love imaginable. I will never forget what I saw. I will never forget how I felt.

My two near death experiences were very different from one another. What I have come to realize is that every person's death experience is unique. It does not mean that just because a loved one does not appear as my mother did that they have not had a blissful transition. I believe that this near death experience was brought to me so that I would understand my mother and what she saw. It was brought to me in this form to comfort me.

Since I have had experiences with my spirit leaving my body, it seems to slip in and out while I am going about my daily business. At times, my spirit longs for the unconditional love that I experienced in the brilliant whiteness. I believe that this feeling is what I innately longed for as a child. I could not understand why some people would deliberately make life difficult, when the potential to recreate the unconditional love here on Earth is very possible. I intuitively knew that there was a place of unconditional love and I longed to return to it.

The Present

Since finishing my Master's Degree in Education Research, I have had time to delve into my passion of understanding the human spirit's potential. When I embarked on my graduate work, I had no intention of focusing on Spirituality in Education. I was quite content with my personal revelations as they emerged throughout my life. In fact, I had not even realized that there were courses on spirituality in the program.

My thesis was on a new government policy, which required teachers to write annual professional growth plans. I was interested in finding out how principals were creating the professional culture for teachers to draft and carry out annual goals. Therefore, much of my course work dealt with change theory and government policy. I had one more course to take to complete my degree.

In the Spring Guide, I discovered a course called *Philosophy of Mind*. It promised to explore the relationship between body, mind and spirit. I really did not have any particular expectations. I only took that particular course because it seemed like a diversion from my immersion in government policy. I was hoping that I would meet a bunch of people who were as curious as I was about discovering the full capacity of the human spirit. In this class, I had the most outstanding vision that I have ever had.

At our first meeting, we were each asked by our professor to speak on why we took the course on the philosophy of body, mind and spirit. In my typically open fashion, I shared my most intense spiritual experiences with the group. In conclusion, I told my classmates that, from time to time, people who are close to death want to talk to me about how to care for their spirits. I told the class, "Every time they ask, I wonder why these people did not take care of their spirits while they were healthy. I want to honor mine every day, not just the few days before my death."

At the end of our first session, our professor gave us a homework assignment – discover how the body, mind and spirit are connected. It never occurred to me to read philosophy or psychology books to derive an answer. I knew of Socrates, Plato and Aristotle. The concepts discovered by Descartes, Sartre and Locke were familiar. Freud and Jung offer interesting theories on the matter. Religions such as Christianity, Buddhism, Islam, Hinduism and Native Canadian beliefs all provide a version of the body, mind and spirit relationship.

Because I had spent numerous years experimenting with how my spirit accesses information, I decided that I was going to let my spirit do my homework for me. I arrived home and immediately got focussed on the task at hand. My children were at their father's house, which left me in quiet surroundings. I closed the living room curtains, unplugged the telephone, got a pad of paper and a pen, turned out all the lights, lit a candle, stretched out on my living room couch and mentally cleared away any distractions in my environment. When I felt centered and calm, when a warm glow formed around the crown of my head, I posed the question, "How are the body, mind, and spirit connected?"

Immediately, the universe responded. The universe does not always speak in clear words as it did when it told me to be a teacher. I received a complete 'knowingness'. As an English speaking human being, my job is to translate the thoughts into something that others can understand. I have done my best. This revelation came as a response to my conscious effort to go into spirit and pull down a truth from the universe. And, now, I feel that I must share this insight that I acquired four years ago.

The theory that I am about to reveal in this book has been my most profound spiritual experience to date. In fact, until I finish this book and begin to present the theory, I feel as though I will not have another spiritual breakthrough. So, is there more to life than what we can grasp with our bodies and minds? Absolutely! With all that has been revealed to me, I can now understand my own human experience in a whole new light. At the urging of my students, who have transformed their lives because of Body, Mind, Spirit, Soul Dominance Theory, I present to you the theory.

PART TWO
Five Aspects of the Human Being

God

Soul

Spirit

Mind

Body

CHAPTER TWO

The Force of Oneness (God) is in All of Us

"Why do we got to hang it on God or Jesus? Maybe," [he] figgered,
"maybe it's all men an' all women we love; maybe that's
the Holy Sperit —the human sperit — the whole shebang.
Maybe all men got one big soul ever'body's a part of.
Now I sat there thinkin' it, an all of a suddent – I knew it.
I knew it so deep down that it was true, and I still know it." [5]

John Steinbeck (1902 – 1968) in *The Grapes of Wrath*

ॐ

Casey, in John Steinbeck's, *The Grapes of Wrath*, is a disillusioned preacher, partly because his own behavior toward women is appalling and partly because he can no longer preach the gospel. He figured out that a holy force connects every human being; that God is not a distant judgmental force, but is inside us, a part of us.

The day that I posed the question, *"How are the body, mind and spirit connected?"* to the spiritual dimension, I found out the same thing.

As soon as I asked the question, an answer came in loud and clear. I was enwrapped in a vision, a complete knowingness that started explaining to me the nature of God, the soul, the spirit, the mind and the body. As the vision unfolded, I was completely amazed, because I could never have conceived of these ideas on my own. The information came so quickly, and there was so much, that it has taken me the last four years to group the information so that I can present it to others.

The vision began by allowing me to understand that there is a single force that radiates through all animate and inanimate beings. It is a Force of Oneness, and all beings are derived from this single force. I could see this force stretching and penetrating like a ray of light into every being. I asked if this Force of Oneness is what people call God. The vision answered, "Yes".

My mind, at the time, pondered how I envisioned God. In my early years, I was taught that God was a male being, very old and very wise, who had silver hair and a long silver beard. He wore a long white robe and lived in heaven. I was told that He watched over us, loved us, and guided us - if we knew how to listen to Him. As I grew older, I viewed God as a benevolent being with whom I was connected. Since I already knew that there were at least two realities, the concept that a God figure was the leader of the spiritual realm made sense to me.

My vision told me, however, that the Supreme Being is a force, a Force of Oneness. While experiencing the 'downloads' the vision presented, I was very much aware that the Force of Oneness (God) was like the pure whiteness I had seen in my second near-death experience. When my spirit came out of my body it felt as if it was becoming fused with the pure whiteness of unconditional love. I can only attempt in Chapter Two to describe the nature of the Force of Oneness by using the images and words that were conveyed to me during my direct experience with it.

The vision explained that there is a Force of Oneness that penetrates each and every one of us and it is through this Oneness that we are all related, no matter what our skin color, religious belief, age, sex, etc. Ultimately, we all have a part of this Force within us, so this means that we all have this aspect of God in us. I am going to call this the God Aspect. We all have a God Aspect. We are all connected through our God Aspect.

This vision conflicted somewhat with what I had been taught all of my life. God was supposed to be a distant being, remote, yet omniscient; a being that was to be revered with wonderment, awe and a sense of foreboding of what might lie in store for me. But, now, I was being shown that which I innately knew all along – that this wise, loving being is actually inside me and everyone else on Earth. In each of us, there is a small droplet of God that penetrates our whole existence, body, mind, spirit and soul. Now I am wondering if I am tapping into my God Aspect when I have my profound moments of 'knowingness'. Maybe we should all learn how to tap into our God Aspect.

Through the Eyes of a Child

When my youngest son was three years old, he told me what happened to him before he was born. I was tucking him into bed, sitting beside him, when he looked up and said, "You know Mom, before I was born, I was sitting beside God and He told me that I had to come down and be a human."

"Really," I said, "What did you say to God?"

"I told Him that I didn't want to come down and be a human because it's too hard. It's nice over there, Mom. I didn't want to come here."

"What did God say?"

"He told me that I had to come. So, I asked Him if I could see my mother and He showed me a picture of you. I told Him that I thought you looked mean and that I didn't want to come."

I admit it. I was a little (okay, a lot) hurt that my son thought that I looked mean. Nevertheless, I tucked those feelings away, and asked again, "What did God say?"

"He told me that I had to come. When God tells you to do something, you do it. So, I got inside your body and when I was born, I looked at your face and thought you are beautiful and I am glad that you are my Mom." He reached up and hugged me in close.

My son says that he does not remember his conversation with God any more. He remembers only the photograph of me that he looked at.

Incidentally, when my son was born, he was breach. The whole delivery was precarious. When he was finally dislodged, through natural childbirth, he was dark blue and not breathing. The cord had been wrapped around his neck the whole three hours of hard delivery. The medical team whisked him away to a table where I heard, "Come on baby, breathe. Come on baby, breathe," for what felt like eternity. At last, a sharp cry relieved all of our worries. Somehow, I wonder if he did not really want to be born and this was his way of getting out of it.

I have told this story to others as a way of explaining that we indeed have been sent to Earth by a divine force. Our life has meaning and purpose. Our job is to figure out what that purpose is and to derive meaning from it. However, on a couple of occasions, parents have been startled by this story. One mother told me that her son reported that he was having conversations with God. She said that she did not pay much attention to his experience, thinking that he was just trying to get attention, or that he had an overactive imagination. But when she heard the story of my son, whom she knew, she wished that she had paid more attention to her own son's relationship with God. This mother was a reporter, and only gave truth credit if it could be proven through rigorous research tools. She discounted her son and he knew it. At the time, he really did not care and replied, "God told me that you wouldn't understand." As her son grew older, he forgot that he had had conversations with God.

Another mother told me that her son, at about the age of three, revealed that God said that his purpose in life is to conquer the bull. He said he was told that he should figure out what that meant before he turned eight because, by then, he would not remember God any more.

These children seemed to be speaking to a person, and referred to Him as a male figure, the one that was in my traditional teachings. At the time of my son's recollection, I had not received the vision, which is central to this book. Therefore, I did not know enough at the time to ask some probing questions like, "Did God speak in words, or was your conversation more of a knowingness?" I did ask him what God looked like. He told me that he could not see God. God was just there.

As a child, I received messages, as I outlined in Chapter One, and in order to convey the messages, I have attached words as if these words were actually used in the transference of the knowledge. With my new understandings of the vision, I am wondering if there are times when we are fused with the Force of Oneness, which is actually what we refer to as God. I am wondering if our cultural consciousness makes sense of this fusion by giving the Force a name of God with human characteristics, with human language.

I remember my son saying to me when he was about seven or eight years old, as he stood over the kitchen sink eating a juicy pear, "Mom, you know what I just discovered? You know how pears grow from a tree. I wonder if in heaven when we are ripe, we fall down to the earth; that the seed God plants is our heart. Oh ya," he said, "God makes something out of nothing." I like this image. After my vision, I believe that God (or the Force of Oneness) is planted inside us; it is the seed of unconditional love, which is the essence of the Force of Oneness.

But why do children forget? My son came home from school one day really angry. He was in grade four at the time and could not tolerate one more day being supervised by the lunchroom staff at his school. He saw them as cruel and vindictive. Trying to reason with him, he looked into my eyes and said, "Mom, you don't get it. They take little grade one kids who see unicorns and rainbows and little leprechauns playing in the grass and turn them into people who see fire and sharp pointed sticks."

As adults, do we steal from our children the magic of God, the beauty, the unconditional love, and force them to see life as hard and miserable? Do we teach them to forget that we are all connected, that we should all feel compassion for one another?

Through the Eyes of an Adult

My vision taught me that this universal Force of Oneness connects us all. Whenever I am preparing to give a presentation, a curious thing happens. First of all, I go into the 'zone' in which I receive insight for my presentation, then I find that every single person that passes me in the street, at the mall, anywhere, looks familiar. I feel related to everyone. Now I am wondering if that is because the Force of Oneness connects each of us. The Natives here in Canada begin their prayers with addressing everyone as "All My Relations" because they know that we are all connected; we are all one.

This revelation of the God Aspect was new to me, but not new to John Steinbeck. His characters in *Grapes of Wrath* must persevere through starvation, discrimination and hopelessness, all because the rich landowners have not figured out as Casey has that we are all one; that we are all a part of the Force of Oneness.

Tom Joad, a main character, decides to carry on the work of Casey, promoting the idea that we are all one, that no one is superior to another. Tom must protect his family by leaving them, since his attempt to save Casey's life left a man dead. The police are searching for him, so in an attempt to alleviate his mother's worry he tells her, "I'll be ever'where – wherever you look. Wherever they's a fight so hungry people can eat, I'll be there. Wherever they's a cop beatin' up a guy, I'll be there. If Casey knowed, why, I'll be in the way guys yell when they're mad an' – I'll be in the way kids laugh when they're hungry an' they know supper's ready. An' when our folks eat the stuff they raise an' live in the houses they build – why, I'll be there."[6] Tom has realized that we are all connected, equal and deserving. He knows, because he can feel the Force of Oneness.

We can experience this 'Oneness' in many ways. Another significant way is to feel an absolute joyful connection with the world around you. For example, I was driving to work one morning, when I paused at a stop sign. A boy, about the age of eight, stood ready to cross the street. He was wearing bright orange pants, and to me they flashed across the street. I admired his daring nature to wear brilliant orange pants to school. Then I thought of him as someone's son, grandson, brother, friend and student. Soon I felt rather choked up at the compassion I felt for this young stranger, thinking that my own children were walking to school at the same time. At that moment, he was my son as I watched him safely cross the street and I sent him the warmest wishes for a long, healthy, happy life. I even wrote a poem about him in my journal book when I arrived at school, because that moment of contact had such a profound impact on me.

I wonder if that is how the Force of Oneness works, if only we would stop our 'busy'ness long enough to feel the connection. Here is a classic example - I needed to turn left at a relatively busy intersection. I was stopped, when suddenly an opening appeared and I got my car halfway into the oncoming traffic lane. Wouldn't you know, an oncoming car swooped in and took the opportunity that I had to make a safe left-hand turn? I slammed on my brakes, but was then left hanging in the oncoming lane. Another car came along and honked at me and the driver glared out the window. Who has not been trapped like this at least once? Thankfully, someone finally let me make my left turn so that I could get out of the way.

At that point, I was everyone. We have all been caught in an awkward situation. Let's have compassion and feel that Oneness. According to my own vision, since we all have a God Aspect to us, then we all have the potential to access this part of ourselves and to access universal truth.

To sum up what I learned about our God Aspect is that it is the part of us that can access universal truth. It is the part of us that is unconditional love, the love that our Spirit Aspect longs for. We are all related to every being, animate and inanimate. We were sent to Earth at this time in history with a divine purpose and sent to a particular family for a reason. Our divine purpose is our Soul Aspect, and it is this aspect that acts as our anchor. It grounds us with a reason for being. For me, my reason for being, my anchor that grounds me is my role as a teacher.

CHAPTER THREE

Our Soul Aspect

Mr. Freeman turns off the wheel and grabs a piece of chalk without washing his hands. "SOUL," he writes on the board. The clay streaks the word like dried blood. "This is where you can find your soul, if you dare. Where you can touch that part of you that you've never dared look at before. Do not come here and ask me to show you how to draw a face. Ask me to help you find the wind." [7]

Laurie Halse Anderson (1961 -) *in Speak*

ॐ

Mr. Freeman is an art teacher in Anderson's novel, *Speak*. His goal is to not only teach his students to draw the mechanics of the human figure, but to inspire them to discover the soul.

My vision taught me what the Soul Aspect of a person actually is. I had always thought that the soul and the spirit were the same things. They are not.

At first the vision showed me that the Force of Oneness (God) splits into an indefinite number of subgroups, commonly referred to as soul groups. Each soul group has a particular purpose to fulfill. Each soul group has an indefinite number of spirits in it, which are all given minds and bodies to carry out the soul purpose and, since we are all connected, our God purpose.

The idea that we all have a soul purpose and that our body is the tool to carry out this purpose is not a new concept. Many philosophers and writers have discovered this concept. If you are particularly interested, you might wish to read Caroline Myss's book *Sacred Contracts*. [8] She understands that we were all put on Earth with a contract to fulfill certain tasks. The people we meet are to help us honor our divine obligation and for us to help them.

The difference between my vision and the ones in the many books that I have read in preparation for this book is that my vision specifically distinguished between our soul and our spirit. I have found that most people use the words soul and spirit as if they are one and the same. My vision told me that there is a definite difference.

Our Soul Aspect is the part of us that has a purpose, what Caroline Myss calls a sacred contract. When I was four years old, a voice in the darkness told me that I was to be a teacher. Being a teacher is my reason for being put on Earth at this point in time in history. No matter how scattered my days can become, I find that being a teacher is my one solid foundation for my life. In fact about four years ago, I had a very mysterious experience.

One morning, I woke up to the sound of my alarm clock, the radio announcers babbling away. I was utterly and completely disassociated with my surroundings. Wide-eyed, I peered around my room, not recognizing anything. I was thinking in pure thoughts, not words, but when I formulated the ideas into words, this is how it translated out.

"What is that noise?" (I was referring to the radio). "I know that humans know what that sound is. They use it for something. It means something to them."

"It means you get up," said a booming male voice, the same one that told me that I had to be a teacher.

"Get up? I know that means something to humans. What is it... get up? Why do I have to do this 'get up' thing?"

Meanwhile, I was looking around my room, not recognizing what my hand was, or the window, or the walls. Everything was completely out of my realm of understanding. I was not afraid, just confused.

"You work," said the voice.

"I work? I know humans do this thing called work. But what does this mean? They use that sound (radio) as a symbol. It tells them to get up and go to work, whatever that means."

"You are a teacher," the voice finally stated.

Suddenly, everything made sense. "I am Margot McKinnon. I am a teacher. Get up means to have a shower and a clock radio is what humans use as their symbol to get up and do their work." I chuckled in my bed, thinking how humans had the funniest symbols to tell them to do things. The last thought I had before I got in the shower was humans need to learn what symbols the spirits use to make contact, for there are human symbols and spirit symbols.

Nevertheless, when I remember this experience, which happened just prior to my vision, I realize that being a teacher is my anchor. It is what pulled me out of my disorientation. It is what reminded me of who I am. I am guessing that my soul called me back. I believe that my spirit went over to a different dimension while I was sleeping and met up with my soul. My alarm clock startled my spirit back into my body and at the time it was confused at being suddenly sucked back into my body and, therefore, could not even recognize anything from the earthly dimension. My soul had to inform my spirit. From this mysterious experience, I can understand what my vision was telling me – our body, mind, spirit, soul and God are different aspects of ourselves. We need to become acquainted with each one.

When I first started to receive the vision, the impression I got was, as I said before, that there is a universal force, which I am calling God because many people recognize that term. God is actually a force, a creator. I imagined that God is like the head coach of a football team and the soul groups are the assistant coaches, each in charge of a different skill set of the team. The soul coach, on behalf of The Force of Oneness (God) is in charge of the spirits who are sitting on the bench, waiting to be put into the game. They are coached on the sidelines, becoming ripe according to my son's pear analogy. When an individual spirit is ready and the timing is right for his skill set, he is sent into the game to fulfill a particular purpose, one that will ultimately serve the whole team, not just himself. Once the spirit is sent in, he is given a task and a body to fulfill the task. While he is playing, he keeps his focus just on the game play, just doing what he has to do. He is not thinking about the head coach, or his assistant coach, or even the ultimate purpose of the team. He is thinking only about fulfilling his particular task.

This football analogy encapsulates how my vision showed that each one of us has been put into the game of life to fulfill a particular game play. However, there are many people toiling away each day, unaware of their purpose. For some, reaching the mid-life years brings about a sense of emptiness. The mid-life crisis, as this stage of life is usually referred to, strikes some people with a profound sense of emptiness. They look around at all of the material possessions that they have accumulated over time and realize that there must be more to life than buying a bigger house, purchasing a faster car, or remaining at a job or in a relationship that is unfulfilling. Suddenly, there is an awakening of the Soul Aspect.

In the younger years, the Soul Aspect may have remained dormant. The excitement of being sent to Earth as a human being was overwhelming. Tasting food again, after being in the spiritual dimension, was exhilarating. Gorging on the tangible parts of the human experience, like shopping for new clothes, playing sports, and even engaging in sexual relationships was magnificent. The old saying, "We are not here for a long time; we are here for a good time," is so true in the sense that the human tangible experience, in which we are given a body, is such a brief moment when compared to our existence as a spiritual being. We come and go from the earthly experience and some people relish every moment. However, for many people when mid-life approaches, they are satiated with the tangible things and begin to long to connect back up with their Soul Aspect. They have been operating for the most part with the Body and Mind Aspects, indulging in the sensory parts of the human experience. When these experiences begin to become less satisfying, the Soul Aspect has room to make an appearance in the human consciousness. We feel a longing for our Soul.

As a high school teacher, however, I have discovered that this longing for the Soul Aspect does not just emerge during mid-life. Teen-agers also have a deep desire to honor their Soul Aspect. When I meet a new group of students, I spend time with relationship building activities. One of them is an activity based on Lewis Thomas' personal essay called *Seven Wonders.*[9] In his essay, he describes a dinner party that he was to attend. Each guest was to bring a list of his or her personal seven wonders. We are all familiar with the concept of the man-made wonders like Stonehenge, the Pyramids, the Hanging Gardens and the Great Wall of China, even if we cannot name all seven. Thomas was an entomologist. Therefore, his list of his personal seven wonders revolved around bugs and bacteria.

My students were asked to make a list of their personal wonders, after which they were to share two of their wonders with the class. A curious thing happened. Some students approached my desk, shyly unfolding their papers to ask if they were allowed to wonder about certain things. Written on their papers were questions like, "Are ghosts real? Is there a God? What is going to happen to me after I die?"

One common wonder with the whole class was, "What is my purpose in life?" I was surprised that the students were nervous about putting such wonders to paper. It was like they were apprehensive about actually being allowed to wonder about the spiritual nature of mankind. I told them, "If that is what you wonder about, then put it down."

When the time came to present their two favorite wonders, invariably the wonders revolved around spirituality, with purpose in life being the most popular. The question about ghosts broke open a loud discussion on ghost stories. Many students had seen a ghost, or had a relative who had seen one. I asked, "What is the difference between a ghost, a spirit and a soul?"

According to my students, a ghost is a spirit that has not moved on to the spiritual dimension. A spirit is the part of us that will move on to heaven, as they called it, after the body dies. A soul, they said, is a higher part of us, the one most closely connected to God. I was astounded, quite frankly, that their interpretation of the spirit and soul so closely aligned with my vision. There were a few students who were doubtful of the existence of God, ghosts, spirits and souls. Most of the students were very sure that the human being has a spirit and a soul. They were curious about what the spiritual dimension was really like. They were concerned about what would happen to them in that spiritual dimension after death.

I was interested in my adolescent students' desire to know their purpose in life. Many of them acknowledged that their ultimate career choice could be decided in terms of the lifestyle they desired, as in a big house, holidays, nice clothes and cars. But they also concurred that a career choice could be determined by whether it fulfilled their purpose in life. Most students wanted to do both. They wanted to fulfill their purpose and make lots of money. It was made very obvious, through this exercise, that teen-agers also struggle with the meaning of life. Their Soul Aspect niggles at them, urging them to follow a purpose. Unfortunately, our school system does not typically teach students how to recognize the Soul Aspects' subtle nudges. Instead, students are left wondering if they are even allowed to think about the spirit or the soul.

Discovering Soul purpose is a key factor to the level of enjoyment in one's life. I find that rejecting negative influences allows me to stay on the path of my purpose. I do not enjoy gossip. I do not like to have negative, toxic people in my life. I do not enjoy taking on tasks that do not give me a sense of pleasure and meaningfulness. The way I see my life is that there are billions of people on Earth. I do not need to spend time with the chronic complainer types. There are a million tasks to be done as well. I will choose the ones that I enjoy and leave the other ones that I do not find so pleasurable for others who do derive pleasure. That does not mean that I pick all of the gemstone tasks. I pick the ones that I like, that others may not like. I like being happy, so I do things that make me happy.

Some people have told me that I live with my 'rose colored' glasses on. They say that I must face the fact that negativity is everywhere. That may well be, but that does not mean that I need to let it seep into my home, my work, or my life. I find that by rejecting negativity, I can hear my Soul Aspect's message. I try to solve chaotic situations quickly so that I can proceed with my purpose. If I can help it, I will not let them get out of hand.

This brings me to the point of addressing the fact that there is evil in our world. I do not want to stay on this negative topic for more than a paragraph, so I will address it quickly and move on. Yes, there is evil. There is a dark side to the spiritual world. Some people, like Hitler for example, have taken up evil purposes. They have listened to the dark side, instead of the light. They either chose to listen to the dark side because they liked the power, or they listened because they were never taught how to push the dark away in order to see the light. Quite frankly, I have found it is much easier to be bad than good. Substance abuse, gossip, lying, and laziness – these are all easier to get caught up in than stepping up and saying, "No!" to these things. However, if we can reject the dark voices that whisper such horrible things like "You're fat", "Take another drink", "Steal it, you want it" etc., then we can reach to a higher level of good. The bottom line on negativity is to reject the negative ideas and longings that will take you away from a meaningful purpose. If a purpose is about hurting someone for whatever reason, then it is dark or evil. If a purpose will help someone, it is most likely a good one.

Students and friends often ask me how to discover soul purpose. Mine came to me when I was four years old, out of the blue. How does a person recognize his or her soul purpose if it is not delivered like mine was? My response to that is to become more conscious. How many whisperings in your ear have you ignored? How many times have you traveled in a certain direction, whether it is in a job or relationship that you knew was wrong for you? Did you hang on for dear life out of obligation or fear? I believe that we can learn our soul purpose by being more conscious of the ideas, or 'knowings' as I call them, that pop into our heads. I even suggest keeping track of these in a journal book. Become more conscious of what your dreams are telling you.

I have found that since I have been studying the Spirit Aspect of ourselves that my birthday has taken on a much bigger significance than presents and cake. It now lasts about two months. I deliberately try to finish all projects by my birthday, like this book for instance. I clear away all clothes that no longer fit my body or my desire, clear away clutter, and on and on. I want to start my new year off fresh. I pay careful attention to my dreams as I move toward my new year. I keep track of the whisperings.

The year that I turned forty, I had a very inspiring dream. In it, I was cleaning my basement stairwell, specifically scrubbing the stairs as part of my birthday cleansing ritual. Suddenly, I noticed a door. I could not believe my eyes. How could there be a door in my house that I had never seen before? I turned the handle and the door swung open to the most magnificent room. It was huge, with floor to ceiling windows on one end, gleaming hardwood floors and enormously high ceilings. There were painter's cloths on the floor as if someone had been fixing it up. "Wow", I thought. "How could I have not known that I had this room in my house? I could have been using it for my eldest son's bedroom." Then I spied another door and it led to another magnificent room with yet another door.

My doorbell rang just then and a friend was there to wish me a happy birthday. I was so excited to show him all of my new rooms. He suggested that we go outside to see how big my house actually was. In reality, I live in a small, three-bedroom bungalow. From the back of my dream house, I could see that it had expanded to three stories high and it extended farther than my eye could see. A beautiful, pink climbing rose grew up the backside. I was amazed. Then I woke up.

I suppose I could have just enjoyed the temporary enjoyment of a dream house. Instead, I chose to interpret the symbolism of it. As my birthday approached, I was clearing away old projects to get ready for a new year, a new decade. My dream represents that there are a lot of doors that I have yet to open, let alone even notice. There are a lot of opportunities that I have missed because I simply did not see them. If I become more conscious, I will see the many doors of opportunity and I will open them. When I do this, my life will be bigger than I ever imagined. I consider this book one of the doors in my dream house. I had the vision, which is seeing the door and now I am persevering in the writing process to formalize the vision, the opening of the door. In the end, my life will have many more doors to open.

What I suggest to anyone searching for their soul purpose is to keep a journal, a record of the whisperings, dreams, coincidences and longings. Soon you will see a pattern and you can become more conscious of your purpose. The problem for many people is that they tend to be too focused on their own immediate task and forget that they are part of a much larger divine purpose. If we really want to fulfill our purpose, however, we must become better acquainted with our Spirit, Soul and God Aspects.

The Soul Aspect Splits

Just as our God Force can split, giving each of us a droplet of the Force of Oneness, our Soul Aspect also splits. There are an infinite number of soul groups, each with its own purpose. The overall soul force splits and is dropped, installed, fused, whatever the appropriate word is, into individuals so that they can fulfill certain tasks on Earth.

What this means is that people who belong to the same soul group share souls. The message showed me a pyramid diagram in which The Force of Oneness was at the top. From this Force were several soul groups, each one with a specific purpose. A brief diagram would look like this.

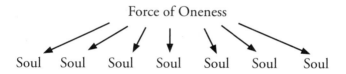

Notice how God or the Force of Oneness gives birth to various souls. The message I got was that each one of these souls has a specific purpose; each is designed so that the individuals who make up the soul group play a part in accomplishing the goals of the Force of Oneness or God.

I must belong to the soul group that is required to nurture children because I am a teacher, a mother and an aunt. Other people who may belong to my soul group might be nurses, pediatricians, social workers, other educators and so on. My brother-in-law belongs to a soul group that nurtures the Earth. His life is about creating renewable energy sources and he has just started a Bio-Diesel company servicing North America. He is fascinated by windmills, solar energy, waste management, organic gardens and anything that falls in line with preserving Earth's infrastructure. He must belong to a soul group with other individuals who are environmentalists such as park rangers, firefighters, scientists investigating pollution, politicians fighting for a clean environment, and so on. Another soul group might ensure that life is fun and colorful - the fashion designers, movie stars, musicians, interior designers, and the like.

From the vision, I realize that I have a piece of a soul inside me that is shared by others. Through the Soul Aspect, I am connected to other like-minded souls, but through the God Aspect, I am connected to everyone on this planet. When we think about it, our daily contact with people is actually quite limited. We may see hundreds of people in a day, but how many of them are actually in our inner circle. There are certain people, whether they are in our family, or in our network of friends and colleagues, with whom we share a special bond. Perhaps these are the ones with whom we share a soul purpose.

Sometimes we find that our family members are not the ones that we feel most connected with. Just because we are in the same family does not necessarily mean that we share a soul, that we are soul mates. But we are still meant to learn something from each other. My son told me that God specifically told him that he had to come to Earth to be my son. I take this quite seriously. He was sent to me for a reason and I was chosen as his mother for a reason. Our job is to figure out what that reason is. There is a purpose behind why we ended up in the same family.

I very often have teen-age students confess to me that they do not know how they ended up in the family that they did. Some of them feel like the parents of their parents. They see their parents going off the rails and these young people try to nurture and guide these adults, by age only, back to some sort of productive living. Perhaps, that is the reason why God sent these young people into the particular families.

The ultimate message that I received is that we share a soul with relatives, friends, colleagues and complete strangers; people who were sent to Earth at this particular time in history to fulfill a particular task. Our job is to remember what this task is. We are also assigned a Spirit Aspect. In the next chapter, I will outline the difference between the Soul Aspect and the Spirit Aspect and expand upon the capabilities of our Spirit Aspect.

CHAPTER FOUR

Our Spirit Aspect

There are more things in heaven and earth, Horatio,
Than are dreamt of in your philosophy.[10]

William Shakespeare (1564 – 1616) in *Hamlet*

෨

In Shakespeare's classic tale, Hamlet is surprised by the appearance of his father's ghost and is not sure if the ghost is real or imagined. He lived in a time period in which most people believed in ghosts, so the visit is not an outrageous experience for him. The problem is that the ghost beckons Hamlet to take revenge upon his death by killing his murderer, the King's own brother. For the rest of the play, Hamlet struggles with understanding the nature of the human spirit.

In my vision, I could see the radiant light of the Force of Oneness dividing into an infinite number of soul groups. Each soul group had a purpose and it divided or branched off into an infinite number of spirit groups. I was surprised to learn that the soul and the spirit are different. The soul is to the spirit what the mind is to the body. The soul drives the spirit, just as the mind drives the body.

I was also surprised to find out that just as we share a soul with others, we share a spirit with others, too. While our Soul Aspect is our purpose, our Spirit Aspect is our desire. It is the part of us that looks just like us, the one for me that came out when I was ill at university and the one that rose up to the place of unconditional love while I was doing the Sundance Ceremony. It is the 'real' us. The soul is a higher version of our spirit; it is the part of us that is closest to God and it is the one with the main reason for our being. Our Spirit Aspect likes to have fun and it longs to be loved and appreciated.

Think about all of the people, activities and things that you desire in life. This is your spirit speaking to you. What I learned about the spirit as a result of my near death experiences is that it longs for absolute and utter unconditional love, the kind that I was a part of in my second near death experience. It wants to be euphoric all of the time. It loves to explore. My spirit sometimes feels confined in my body. I can feel when it gets restless because I become exhausted - incapacitated by fatigue. It wants me to lie down, so that it can roam to distant landscapes, knowing that my body is safe and secure in my bed.

For me, exhaustion is internal desire versus external pressure. What I mean by this is my desires of spirit are not being met because of physical, 'real life' restrictions, like I have to go to work, or I have to pay all of my bills, or I have to sit through a lesson on financial planning, or I have to take care of breakdowns in my house. Even though I love my job as a schoolteacher, sometimes it gets in the way of me finishing this book. My spirit and soul really want me to complete this project, but the eight hours that I spend at work and the two hours of marking in the evening, at times, prevents me from fulfilling my obligation to my soul. And my spirit delights in writing this book. I can only imagine how horrible it must be for those people who must go to a job every day in which their spirit and soul are not delighted.

I have come to realize that my spirit will not only leave my body when I die, but it has the ability to leave my body while I am alive. Imagine that you decided to vacation all by yourself on the sunny beaches of Mexico. You left all of your troubles of work and home behind and gave your spirit a holiday. Every day you lay on your towel, reading your favorite vacation book – taking time every once in a while to cool off with a dip in the ocean. Your only trouble was to decide what you were going to have for lunch or dinner.

Evening came. After a luxurious shower, you strolled through the tropical garden to the outdoor patio for dinner. The glowing orange and pink sunset was a perfect companion for the first few evenings. But one evening, a solitary suntanned traveler sat at the very next table. Drawn to each other, you both decide to share a table. Immediately a connection was made. Soon you were laughing and sharing secrets. The sun started to rise and still you were enraptured in each other's company. For the rest of the holiday, you and this spirit mate were inseparable.

The inevitable arrived. It was time to pack up and return to real life. Upon arrival home, instead of euphoria, you felt empty, despondent, lonely and miserable. Your spirit was still on the Mexican shore, wandering hand in hand with your spirit mate. Nothing in real life brought enjoyment. You got to the bottom of the stairs to the basement and could not remember what you went down there for. At a dinner party, you were only there in body. Your spirit, lonely for the joy stimulated by your newfound love, left you only with a fraction of your will power.

What really happened is this — because your spirit is independent, it had left your body and soared off into the spiritual dimension. There was a total disconnect between body, mind and spirit.

We often hear of rape victims who are never the same after their vicious attack. A friend of mine told me that she could never marry or have children because every time she got close to a man, she could see the face of her rapist. At that time, she was nearing her fiftieth birthday. I told her how the spirit could get stuck in time. Her spirit stayed in its eighteen year old form, on that tragic evening when the next-door neighbor attacked her. I taught her how to retrieve her spirit from that terrible time in her life. Sometimes our spirit will stick, like Velcro, to a person or place. It resists moving forward. I liken the retrieval process as ripping apart strips of Velcro. Sometimes we have to use all of our might to pull our spirit away from the past and bring it into the present.

My friend needed her spirit, her desires in life, to help guide her to her soul purpose. She needed to find some meaning to her attack, then call her spirit by her own name and tell it to come back into her body. Then she needed to learn how to treat her body better, as she tended to overuse alcohol and even smoked marijuana to alleviate the pain of her past.

When I finished telling her about her spirit, I saw tears streaming down her cheeks. She had missed her spirit terribly and had never realized that this is why she felt so empty. She did call her spirit back and created a nicer temple (body) for her spirit to live in. To top it off, she even ended up getting married.

A student in my class became very despondent. Her eyes had lost their sparkle and she no longer participated in class routine. I asked her to meet for lunch to talk about what was going on. She revealed that something had happened and that she felt empty. She also said that she was not treating herself very well and now she was really sad. I told her the same thing that I told my friend, that her spirit had left her body because it did not want to live there any more. This made sense to her. I asked her what her favorite meal was and she said lasagna, Caesar salad and garlic bread. I recommended that she make this dinner and talk to her spirit, telling it the specific ways that she was going to clean up her life. She was to invite her spirit to come back into her body and, in return, she was going to honor her body more. The dinner was a signal to the spirit that she wanted to improve her total quality of life. The next day, she arrived smiling and her eyes had their sparkle back. "It worked!" she said.

Most of us have fallen madly in love with another person's spirit. We know that we should not love this person because they live in another country and the relationship could never work, or he/she is married, or he/she is too old or too young. There are countless reasons. I watched the recent release of the film *Brokeback Mountain*. The main character, Ennis, falls in love with his work partner, Jake. Ennis is tormented by his feelings of absolute love for his male friend. For unexplainable reasons to him, he loves Jake and, as a result, cannot fully function as a husband and father to his wife and two little girls, whom he adores. Ennis's spirit loves Jakes' spirit, regardless of the Body Aspect, the fact that they are both males.

Ultimately, what I learned from my vision is that the spirit is our desire, and that it will leave our body if we do not create a life in which it wants to live. How many people are walking around with 'dead eyes' and miserable attitudes because they are employed at jobs that they hate, or have stayed too long in a marriage that is not working? We must create a life in which our spirit wants to stay in our body to go along for the ride. It is defeating our purpose to create a life in which the spirit feels as though it is in a prison. Listen to your spirit and make changes to your lifestyle when necessary.

The importance of understanding that the soul and the spirit are different became very obvious to me. The spirit is not perfect. It can get us into a lot of trouble. If we start having extra-marital affairs because our spirit has fallen in love with and desires another's spouse, we can hurt a lot of people. We need to recognize if this love relationship is one that will bring us closer to, or farther away, from our soul purpose.

Our spirit can be feisty and take us in a direction that may not align with our soul purpose. It may become confused because of its many desires and be downright naughty. I found out that it is so important for us to become more conscious of our soul's purpose, our anchor, so that our spirit can connect with it.

The impression that I got during my vision was one that I can only describe as a platform diver who dives directly into the swimming pool. When he hits the bottom, he dolphin kicks his way to the surface of the pool. As human beings, our soul 'dolphin' kicks through our body, up through our mind, rises above spirit and then at the very surface of the water gulps in the life force of God. This is how I felt when I had my second near-death experience, as if I was gulping in the life force of God.

Somehow, I got the impression that as an earthly incarnated person, our body, mind and spirit are the most active. The soul dimension, while inside of us, is the string that connects us to the Godly dimension. It is stable. If I go back to my diving analogy, the soul 'dolphin' kicks at the bottom of the 'pool' through the Body Aspect. It must rise above physical pain, hunger and distress in order to reach a higher level. It must then enter the Mind Aspect and rise higher still, through jealousy, hurt, poor self-esteem, anger and more human weaknesses. It enters the Spirit Aspect and must transcend the Spirit Aspect's desires, like having an affair, sleeping all day, or abandoning all human responsibilities, in order to reach the soul purpose. When the soul rises up through the Body, Mind, and Spirit Aspects, it can gulp in the life force of God (The Force of Oneness). The soul is our reason for being and we must not succumb to the foibles of the body, mind, or spirit if we intend on actualizing this purpose. My soul is what reminds me why I was put on this Earth in the first place – to be a teacher. My spirit comprises of all the desires that I have here on Earth.

The Spirit Splits

Just like the soul splits, so does the spirit. We can share the same spirit with several people. I created another diagram that hopefully will demonstrate how each aspect of ourselves has split and how we share our aspects with others. I will show you what was conveyed to me. I have limited the diagram to showing just three soul groups and only eight spirit groups. Imagine that there is actually an indefinite number of soul and spirit groups. There is only one God, or Force of Oneness.

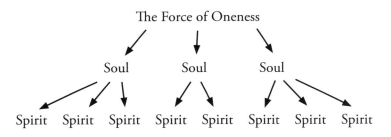

What the voice revealed to me is that one human being can share a spirit with another human being. The spirit, because it is immaterial, can split just like the Soul Aspect and the God Aspect. Two or more people may share the same spirit. We feel as if we are almost the same person because we have so much in common. This explains why we may feel like we have known someone forever, even though we just met. This is a kindred spirit. We can also share a mind with other people and may feel that we have the same mindset, which I will demonstrate in the next chapter. The body that we are given is the only tangible. Procreating and having children divide it. The body is the tool for the mind, spirit and soul.

What I found quite remarkable is that the spirit can divide, or split, even when it is inside of us. Parts of our spirit can get stuck in a time or place. It can get stuck on a person whom we loved or a person who hurt us. Chapter Nine explores the characteristics of a Spirit Dominant person. Some people, without realizing it, have a very active Spirit Aspect. I outline the temperament of Spirit Dominant individuals, which demonstrates the effects of the spirit's ability to leave the body and wander at will. Our Spirit Aspect plays a role in every part of our life and is so much more than most of us realize.

The most fascinating revelation I received from my vision is that the soul and spirit are not the same and that the soul and spirit can split. This concept explained to me why sometimes I feel divided, only part of myself. I felt that I understood better why I sometimes feel lonesome. What I am really lonesome for is my spirit, because it is stuck somewhere. Although the idea of ripping my spirit away from a past event or a person may sound like a harsh way of putting into words the idea of a stuck spirit, I find that I need to be this assertive with my spirit. My spirit loves to fly around and visit all sorts of people and places, but to be at my best, I need it to stay in my body, whole and powerful. I need it to help me make the decisions that will keep me on the path of my Soul Aspect.

In Chapter Five, I will reveal what my vision told me about the difference between the Spirit Aspect and the Mind Aspect. For most of my life, I was unaware that there was a difference. I now realize that I could have made better choices in my life if I had understood earlier how to discern between knowledge ascertained through my Mind Aspect and that which I gained through my Spirit Aspect.

CHAPTER FIVE

Our Mind Aspect

And yet they look just like ordinary bacteria. Under the electron microscope they have the same essential structure – cell walls, ribosomes, and all. If they were, as is now being suggested, the original archebacteria, ancestors of us all, how did they or their progeny ever learn to cool down? I cannot think of a more wonderful trick.[11]

Lewis, Thomas (1913 – 1993) in his personal essay *Seven Wonders*

᠍ↄ

Lewis Thomas in his *Seven Wonders* essay demonstrates how the Mind Aspect operates. Our Mind Aspect is the part of us that organizes the tangible parts of life. Through the five senses, it shapes and makes sense of the earthly world. It does not tap into the spiritual dimension; our Spirit Aspect does. We all have five layers, or versions of ourselves. In the diagram below, you can see that each spirit divides into mind groups and is eventually given a Body Aspect in order to function on Earth. In a diagram, the message I received looked like this.

Notice in the diagram that in this one particular soul group, there are three spirit groups. Imagine that this diagram is a continuation of all the previous diagrams. There is an indefinite number of mind groups, but my page can only hold so much information. These three spirit groups share a soul. Spirit group one, on the left, has three mind groups, while spirit group two in the middle has four. In reality, spirit groups can divide into an indefinite number of mind groups. I have spent most of my life exploring the potential of my Spirit Aspect and, inadvertently, my soul. My vision outlined how my spirit and mind were different. They each had a different task to fulfill and their messages came in different forms.

After the vision, I began to experiment in an attempt to discern more clearly between my Spirit and Mind Aspects. Both spoke to me, but which one was which? I played around with activities that would assist me in becoming more conscious as to whether information that I received came through my Mind Aspect or my Spirit Aspect. Remember that the spirit embraces our desires. Our mind has a much more limited capability than the spirit. It can only organize what it sees, hears, smells, tastes and touches. It knows how to calculate and measure. It can hypothesize, set up an experiment, use the five senses to collect data, organize the data and confirm or discard the original theory.

When I came up with the Body, Mind, Spirit, Soul Dominance Theory, I was excited to present it to my *Philosophy of Mind* classmates. It so happened that my birthday was nearing, so I selected that day to give my final presentation, since one of my birthday rituals is to finish all incomplete projects. I told the class that I was baking a cake to celebrate. What an undertaking that turned out to be! At first, I thought that I should make a poppy seed cake, but decided not to because most likely I would end up doing my whole presentation only to find out when I got home that I had a poppy seed stuck between my front teeth throughout my great project finale. I chose a layered bundt cake instead. There must have been five different bowls involved. I seemed to be mixing and pouring and washing and remixing. The whole thing was very complicated. Exasperated, I finally looked up and said, "Why did I choose a cake this hard?"

I got an unexpected answer... "Your whole presentation is based on the theory that the human is made up of five layers, body, mind, spirit, soul and God. That is why you made a layer cake. It is a symbol."

My puny little mind only thought about the poppy seed caught in my front teeth and the embarrassment that would ensue. My Spirit Aspect conveyed to me that I was actually building a model for my theory.

Another way that I can think about how to discern between my mind and spirit is through my daily jogging. When my body starts to fatigue, my mind tells me to stop, or slow down, or go home. My mind responds to my physical self by providing an immediate solution, to stop. My spirit tells me to rise above the pain and go into the zone of my spirit's desires. My spirit roams around to all of the places it likes, a beautiful home that I would love to build on a cliff above the Atlantic Ocean, renovations that I would like to do to my home, or some other excursion that it wants to go on. My body continues to run from memory. Before I know it, I am home... pain free.

Another example that I will offer to demonstrate the difference between how my mind works and how my spirit functions is the time that I could not open the padlock on my garden shed. I had just bought the little bungalow that I now live in. In the garden was a shed that housed the lawn mower and garden tools. There was a padlock on it that was not actually locked. It just hung there. I told my children not to lock it because I did not have a key to open it. We just made it look like it was locked.

One day I decided that the lawn needed mowing, so I went to the shed and I could not believe my eyes. The lock was LOCKED! I rummaged through the house to see if the previous owners had left behind any small keys to open it. I found several and tried them, all to no avail. Days of searching went by. The lawn kept getting longer. My mind decided that I needed to purchase a lock cutter. Off I went to the hardware store to buy some sort of metal cutter. It would have taken me until next summer to cut the lock off. The lawn was now embarrassingly long. My mind even wanted to find out who the culprit was that made my life difficult by locking the lock. Of course, none of my three children did it and blaming was not going to help the situation.

Finally, feeling hopeless, I fell to my knees, held the lock in my hands and said, "I have done everything humanly possible to get this lock off. Please help me." Quite honestly, I was not expecting a response, but one came nevertheless. "Your house key opens the lock." I could not believe my ears. I ran into the house, grabbed my house key, held the lock once again, put the key in and, like magic, the lock clicked open.

What I have found out is that I use my mind to figure out how to solve problems in the human world: how to fix things, how to bake, how to get a presentation organized, how to do an endless host of intellectual activities. When I have done all that is humanly possible, I call on my spirit to interact with a spiritual dimension to give me greater insight. That is what I did to find the answer to my professor's question in class – "How are the body, mind and spirit connected?"

Both the Mind and the Spirit Aspects are of equal importance. The Mind Aspect has the ability to make sense of the tangible, physical aspects of life. I have developed my Mind Aspect, but it has a long way to go yet. I still have to give myself half an hour of getting lost time when I am asked to arrive at an unfamiliar location. My mind is not strong enough to pick up the visual clues to know whether I should turn right or left at certain intersections. Giving me East and West directions sends me into a complete intellectual chaos. How am I supposed to know whether I am going East or West?

I found out about four years ago that when I draw a map for someone that I am to put North at the top. This had never occurred to me. A friend was trying to make his way to my house and my instruction was to find 24th Street and then wiggle wag his way to my house, until he found my street, as I live on numbered street, not a named street. This meant that he could locate my house by negotiating through the numbers. "Wiggle wag," he said, "that is your instruction?" It made perfect sense to me.

Math is incomprehensible to me. I stopped at about grade three understanding any reasoning behind it. Fixing broken items in my house is left to my teen-aged daughter. She has a knack for knowing exactly how an object is put together. At age seven, she put my whole barbeque together. I rely on her because her Mind Aspect is so strong. Tangible objects seem so foreign to me – so beyond my realm of knowledge.

My Spirit Aspect is more naturally developed than my Mind Aspect. But, I now know that I share a Mind Aspect with others. We think similarly, make decisions similarly and draw conclusions similarly. I was given a Spirit Aspect of desires, a Soul Aspect of purpose and a God Aspect to recognize the Force of Oneness. In Chapter Six, I will delve into the Body Aspect, which we were also assigned when we were incarnated onto Earth.

CHAPTER SIX

Our Body Aspect

I envy them being able to go to the health club, or go for a swim.
Or dance. Mostly for dancing.[12]

Mitch Albom (1958 -) in *tuesdays with Morrie*

↬

The human body is a remarkable creation. The tiny face of a newborn baby is miraculous. Just the idea that we have eyes that are designed to register the view of a mountain range is incredible. The fact that our tongue has four centers to access the taste of salty, sweet, sour, or bitter foods, and as a result we can enjoy our cravings for a hamburger topped with sweet pickles, Dijon mustard, and fresh tomato is a wonder in itself. Our body has muscles that we can develop in order to perfect a golf swing, or lift our toddler onto our hip. We have even been designed with pleasure centers to thoroughly enjoy the sexual experience.

Mitch Albom in *tuesdays with Morrie* tells the story of Morrie Schwartz's final reflections of the importance of living while he is preparing to die. He begins to envy those who are still members of the land of the living, because he knows that he has only a few months left to be human. Soon he will be bodiless, a spirit that can no longer dance the tango with his beautiful wife, or feel the cool water on his skin while he swims his daily lengths in the pool. He recognizes that our stay on Earth is precious because it is so brief.

The rest of us may very well take the human experience for granted. We enjoy styling our hair, shopping for a new dress for a special occasion, or sitting down for a meal with a sumptuous glass of red wine. But do we let the tangible, physical, body experience soak in? Do we relish and savor the sights and sounds of our every day life?

The human body is an exquisite creation. Some peoples' bodies are lithe and athletic. Stretching to scoop a tennis ball out of the back left corner is done with such grace and dexterity. Weaving through a maze of clawing hands on a basketball court is done with accurate measured steps. Yet, other bodies are not so agile. There are those bodies in an aerobics class that consistently move left when everyone else's moves right. Hands go up when the rest come down. We also notice that some bodies, by society's estimation are more beautiful than others. Some bodies are more hearty and vigorous than others. Some bodies appear to be noticeable, while others are less so, or even virtually invisible.

In the context of a discussion of the God, Soul, Spirit, Mind and Body Aspects, we can easily understand that the body is the visible part of ourselves. It can access the physical, tangible parts of the human experience. Our Body Aspect uses all the body parts as well as the five senses, to interact at a very physical level with the environment around it.

At a soul level, the body is the tool to carry out the soul's purpose. For me, my soul purpose is to teach. My body is the tool I have used to get to school on time, to purchase the necessary materials in order to do well in school and to physically fill in the application forms to get into Teacher's College. I used my mind to study and make sense of the material that I was expected to learn. I used my Spirit Aspect to recognize that I thoroughly enjoyed the study of English literature, that I valued the lessons from English courses more than I did the others and that my desire was to be an English teacher.

What I realized through my vision was that my body is more than just a container for the spirit; it is more than just a tool to serve my Spirit, Soul and God Aspects. As a child, I used to find it extremely exhausting lugging a body around all day. Breathing even seemed like an arduous task. I was a physical, active child, as I mentioned earlier, but I have to say that if I were given a choice between playing a game of soccer and lying on my bed and letting my spirit soar, I would select the latter. My vision taught me to take more pleasure in the human physical 'body' experience.

The body is more than just a tool to fulfill our divine obligation. It is also supposed to be a source of pleasure as well.

The down side of having a body is that it does get tired, it can get injured and it is susceptible to illness. About ten years ago, just after my divorce, I was lying on my bed when I was overcome with the impression that I should give myself a breast examination. My mother was suffering from breast cancer at the time and, therefore, this critical illness penetrated my mind. My right breast felt normal, so I moved on to the left. I was stunned to feel two hard jagged nodules fused to my ribs. I booked an appointment with my doctor for the next day. She diagnosed the lumps as suspicious. A mammogram was scheduled two weeks later. That meant that I had a two week window of opportunity to heal myself.

After the doctor's visit, I lay back on my bed, sent my consciousness up into the spiritual dimension and asked, "Body, why have you decided to get sick?" The answer was, "Because you don't take care of yourself very well. You run yourself ragged. You rarely do anything nice for yourself. I don't like living in this body any more, so I'm leaving."

At that point, I knew that my spirit was talking to me. My Spirit Aspect, which is intangible, was telling me that it wanted to leave because it did not like living in my body any more. The existence that I had created for my spirit to live in was not acceptable, so my spirit was leaving. Ultimately, my body would have to deteriorate and leave too. I asked my spirit, "If I take better care of myself and make your human experience more pleasurable, will you stay?" "Yes," it answered.

I got off my bed, went down to my basement bathroom, which had a beautiful claw foot bathtub. I filled it with warm water and added luxurious scented sea salts. I lit candles and soaked in there until I felt that I had washed away the negativity that surrounded me. Later, I went off to the grocery store and bought nutritious foods that were all my favorites. When my three elementary school-aged children got home, I told them that I was not feeling very well and that I was taking two weeks off. They could make their own breakfasts and lunches. We could watch our favorite videos and read books. I was off duty and there was to be NO fighting. I still went to work, but I slept whenever I felt like it, once I was home. Within a day, the nodules were gone. By the time I went for the mammogram, I was confident that I would get a good report.

My point is that inasmuch as I feel that my Soul purpose is to be a teacher and I live a relatively spiritual way of being, I cannot neglect my Body Aspect. My spirit came to Earth, into my body to enjoy the human experience, to relish in sensual pleasures. Sometimes, I look down at my hands and see my mother's hands. I actually feel as though I am my mother. I get the feeling that my mother has just dropped inside my body to have a few seconds of the human experience. She misses it sometimes. Have you ever felt as though you were somebody else, even for just a few seconds?

The Body Aspect does, from time to time, become injured. When I was delivering my third son, the one that was breach, the doctor was noticeably anxious. The warning signals on the monitors attached to me were flashing and buzzing like crazy and an emergency delivery was obvious. The nurses and doctors tried to talk me through the procedure, when I finally said to them, "You take care of my body and I'll take care of myself," which to me meant that I would go into my Spirit Aspect where I did not have to feel any pain. Before that, I was listening to the doctors with my Mind Aspect and because of it I was fearful. My biggest worry was that they would have to do a caesarian section – without anesthetic, as that is what happened to one of my prenatal classmates. Scary – I had no intention of going there! I remember elevating my spirit out of my body, feeling very calm and peaceful. Finally when Alex was born, I settled my spirit back into my body.

When Alex was in grade three, a car hit him as he was crossing the street. His sister and I got him off the road and moved him to the sidewalk. It was a winter night, on a narrow street and when the ambulance arrived, the paramedics began their work. They asked Alex a lot of questions in order to ascertain his condition. It was clear that his leg was broken and that he had a head injury. Fear started to set in for Alex. I knew it was just his mind talking, so I knelt over him and said, "Alex, look me in the eyes. Raise yourself up and meet me in the eyes." He knew that this meant taking his spirit up and leaving his body on the ground so that the paramedics could work on cutting off his winter boots. He suddenly became very calm and peaceful and he kept his eyes locked on mine. I heard one of the paramedics saying, "Look at this boy. I have never seen someone this young, so calm at a time like this. He is incredible!"

I attempt to give my children spiritual tools to access, so that if ever they find themselves in a situation that makes them panic, they can find the peacefulness of the spirit to overcome the temporary stress. Everyone needs to know that they have a Body Aspect, a Mind Aspect, a Spirit Aspect, and a Soul Aspect that they can access depending on the situation. Everybody needs to learn how to transcend bodily pain, surpass a tangled mind and rise up into spirit and soul to view the grander picture of their situation.

Now that I know I have these five aspects, I tap into each dimension before I make any important decisions. I know that many of you might be asking at this point – "How do I tap into these five aspects?" Just by knowing they exist is a starting point to tapping in. The Spirit Aspect has so many capabilities, just as the body and the mind have. Very few people, though, have experimented with what the capabilities of the human spirit actually are. However, the vision also told me that there is a down side to having an overly developed Spirit Aspect.

In Part Three, I will develop the idea that we are born Dominant in one of the aspects: Body, Mind, Spirit, or Soul. I was born Soul Dominant which means that my Soul Aspect was more developed than my Body or Mind. However, my Spirit Aspect is so active that at times I feel I am Spirit Dominant. In this section, I will outline both the positive and negative characteristics of the Body, Mind, Spirit, Soul Dominant personality types and offer suggestions for remaining in balance.

PART THREE

The Body, Mind, Spirit, Soul Dominance Theory

CHAPTER SEVEN

The Body, Mind, Spirit, Soul Dominance Theory

And when we die
All's over that is ours; and life burns on
Through other lovers, other lips," said I,
"Heart of my heart, our heaven is now, is won!"
We are Earth's best, that learnt her lesson here.
Life is our cry. We have kept the faith!" we said.[13]

Rupert Brooke (1887 – 1915) in his poem *The Hill*

༄

"How are the body, mind and spirit connected?" As I posed this question to the spiritual dimension, that Friday afternoon four years ago, the answers continued to come in loud and clear. I was surprised to find out that we have five aspects to us. I knew that I had a body and a spirit because my experiences told me so. But now this vision was showing me that we are, in fact, encased in these five layers and we can access any particular layer depending on what function we need it to do. But most people do not know this. This part of the vision led to an even more astounding revelation.

What I found out is that we are born dominant, or stronger, or more developed in one of the aspects. Some people are born Body Dominant, others are Mind Dominant, still others are Spirit Dominant, and some are even Soul Dominant. The vision did not reveal God Dominance. We are composed, to varying degrees, of all five. But one particular aspect will always stand out more predominantly than the others. The vision went on to describe the personality traits exhibited by individuals born Body, Mind, Spirit, or Soul Dominant.

My initial reaction to the theory presented to me that remarkable Friday afternoon four years ago was one of gratitude, for it explained to me why I behave the way I do. I considered myself Spirit Dominant at first. I could see how my Spirit Aspect was stronger and more engaged than my body or mind. My Body Aspect seems a bit of a nuisance sometimes, because it is so cumbersome compared to my Spirit Aspect. My Mind Aspect, simply put, is puny. What I can perceive through my mind is so small compared to what I perceive through my spirit.

But as the vision unfolded, I began to think that maybe I was more the Soul Dominant type. My mind, however, interjected and said, "Who do you think you are to consider yourself Soul Dominant? Only gurus and geniuses are Soul Dominant. You are just Margot McKinnon, a mom and a school teacher." Over the last four years, I have certainly embraced my Spirit Aspect and I have had a lot of fun discovering its many desires and aspirations. But what keeps me going, what keeps me motivated during hard times is my soul's purpose – *to be a teacher*.

When I thought that I had finally finished this book and was at the stage of proofing it for typos, I asked, "What is next?" The voice came through to say that since I have embraced my Body, Mind and Spirit Aspects, I would begin the journey to understand my Soul Aspect better – my purpose, my reason for being. I am convinced now that I am Soul Dominant because my purpose to be a teacher has anchored me here on Earth. I have known since I was four years old what my purpose is and I feel a tremendous commitment to my promise to fulfill it. I am thoroughly excited now that I will soon be launched into a journey to explore my Soul Aspect better.

Before I can begin this exciting adventure, I must finish writing this book and teach others how they can recognize if they are Body, Mind, Spirit, or Soul Dominant. I must show the healthy and unhealthy aspects of being a particular dominance and illustrate how individuals can recognize when they are out of balance and how they can bring themselves back into alignment. One thing that I have learned for sure is that being Spirit or Soul Dominant is no more important, no better, no worse than being Body or Mind Dominant.

Each personality type has its unique set of pros and cons. At all times, each of us has access to all five aspects. The vision made it clear to me, however, that we rely on one particular aspect more often than the others in our interaction with our environment. What we need to learn as human beings is that because we are highly developed in one aspect, then it is in our best interest to begin to develop the other four aspects. In times of stress and anxiety, we can alleviate a lot of pain and bring more joy into our lives if we know how to draw upon all five aspects as tools.

The other intriguing part of this theory was that it explained to me why my three children are so different, even though they have been given very similar parenting. I realized, over the course of the revelation, why my marriage broke down. I recognized the various personality types in my students. I could see why some were getting into drugs, why some were cutting or maiming themselves, why some were on every sports team and why some were so focused on their academic achievement.

This theory changed my life. I feel like a veil has been lifted. The following chapters will outline how the Body, Mind, Spirit and Soul Dominance Theory works. They will describe how to recognize and identify the different personality traits of each dominant aspect and will reveal the implications and intricacies of dealing with each of these dominant aspects.

CHAPTER EIGHT

Body Dominance

What is life?
It is a flash of a firefly
In the night.[14]

Crowfoot (1821 – 1890) Blackfoot Chief in his poem *Farewell*

࿊

Crowfoot knew that our time on Earth is but a brief and fleeting moment when he wrote his poem *Farewell* as he was dying. We are given a body to use as a tool with which to experience the physical for what truly is, in the grand scheme of things, but a moment in time. How many of us truly appreciate, value and revel in the human experience, in the exquisiteness of being human?

From Part One, I established that the body is the physical manifestation of ourselves. All that we have to do is look around and see the variety of sizes, shapes, and colors to know that each individual human being interacts with the world with a unique body composition. I am 5'11" tall, with light brown hair and brown eyes. My sisters are around 5'6", my mother was only 5'5" and I passed my father in height by the time I was twelve. Despite looking exactly like the rest of my family and sounding just the same on the telephone, I have often wondered why I am so much taller than my parents and my sisters. What purpose is my height supposed to have? To this day, I do not know. But as a child, I often wondered why I was given such a long, tall body.

The Body Aspect has always featured prominently in our lives. How many of you as parents have held a newborn baby, checking your child over lovingly to make sure he/she was 'perfect', with ten fingers and ten toes? You may also remember checking, as this baby grew, if your child met the development charts. Were they the right height and weight for their age category? Did they crawl and walk at the appropriate times? Did you happen to notice that some babies were walking at nine months while others were still lying on their bellies? Did you watch your child in the playground and notice some were more agile and more coordinated than others? Or at the soccer field – did some children seem to be at one with the soccer ball, running up the midfield, maneuvering through the other children, blasting off the winning goal? What about baseball? There are those children who can whack the baseball through outstretched mitts and run from base to base, scoring a homerun almost every time they are up to bat. But what about the other children who stand at the home plate, never even attempting to make a swing? We realize that some children are natural athletes, while others seem to be interested in other things, in reading or playing with bugs in the dirt, or totally engrossed in imaginary play.

What about the children who love to dress up in their favorite clothes, the ones who love to get haircuts, get gelled up, or primp their hair in perfect pigtails? Their clothes are perfectly coordinated; nails are tidy and shoes are shiny. Then there are some other children with their shirttails hanging out, dirt around the cuffs and hair sticking out every which way.

My vision explained the reasoning behind all this. Some people are Body Dominant. Their Body Aspect is highly developed. A Body Dominant person interacts with the world in a very physical way. They enjoy the sensual pleasures of the human experience. They thrive on sports activities, enjoy their food and have a knack for picking out the best shirt to go with their carefully ironed pants. As adults, Body Dominant people receive great enjoyment from luxurious spa treatments like massage, steam showers and manicures.

A Body Dominant person might assume that everybody loves food. But not everyone does. Only since I discovered this theory, have I taken any interest in food, or in my tangible physical surroundings. I could have ripped off two lettuce leaves and eaten them straight out of my hand and called it a salad. I could go all day without eating because, quite frankly, food and presentation of food is not high on my priority list. But for Body

Dominant people, like my sister, mealtime is an event. She knows exactly how to create a visually pleasing and sumptuous dinner. I actually go into a panic when I have to put on a dinner party for her because I know full well that my sense of taste and smell is not as acute as hers. I do not have a lot of interest in presentation, but I am learning because I now realize that it is important to Body Dominant people.

Body Dominant people notice the fine details of their environment. They find pleasure in discovering the perfect pillow that matches the fleck of green in the curtains. They spend time and money on fine furnishings and the latest technology. Since their physical world gives them so much pleasure, they need to keep it organized and clean, not just tidy, but clean. Everything should have its place. Clutter and items in disrepair aggravate the Body Dominant. They are excellent at having a place for everything. They enjoy the details of physical objects, like textures and colors of fabrics, shapes of buildings and garden designs. Shopping for these objects typically brings great pleasure to Body Dominant people. They enjoy selecting the perfect shade of lipstick for an outfit, or the unique design of a tie to match the thread of a suit jacket. They keep on top of fashion trends.

Being adept at sports, Body Dominant individuals have an overwhelming desire to engage in some sort of exercise regime on a daily basis. Often, they do not understand how everyone does not tend to their bodies as they do. They care very much for their physical appearance as well. Their hair and make-up are carefully maintained; their clothing is pressed and they wear the latest fashions. For men, they may take great pleasure in grooming their facial hair into some unique or trendy style.

Body Dominant people enjoy the sensual aspects of the human experience, like the taste of food, the changing fashion trends and interior design. Capable of creating the most exquisite meal, or hitting the baseball out of the park, or designing a magazine ready bedroom, Body Dominant people really know how to savor the physical, tangible, sensual aspects of the human experience. Achievement to a Body Dominant individual is recognized by something that can be seen, tasted, touched, smelled, or heard. A large, beautifully decorated home, a magnificent car, tidy children, sports awards, anything that is tangible, signifies success to a Body Dominant person.

The following points encapsulate the essence of the Body Dominant individual.

Body Dominant Characteristics

- Appreciates the sights, sounds, tastes, textures and smells of life
- Typically a natural athlete
- Enjoys improving the appearance of objects, like home decorating, gardening, or cleaning the house or vehicle
- Likes to keep all possessions in an organized form, the refrigerator is organized, papers are filed, car is immaculate
- Becomes frustrated at other people's lack of cleanliness, or organization
- Values possessions and likes to have the latest gadgets, or fashion items
- A priority is placed on physical appearance, hair style, make-up, physique, fashion, waxing, tweezing, cosmetic surgery

The Negative Side of the Body Dominant

Body Dominance to the extreme, however, can be quite unhealthy. Some Body Dominant people become obsessed with organization, cleanliness, or immaculate personal appearance. They can work out excessively, to the point of physical injury, or they might resort to numerous sessions of plastic surgery to correct what they perceive as imperfections in appearance. Often they are hyper-critical of others' 'imperfections'; they notice chipped nail polish, dust on the molding, or how messy an office space may be – according to their standards. They may chastise neighbors for not mowing the lawn to perfection, or condemn a daughter-in-law for not keeping an immaculate home. They may not understand why everyone does not want to join in the 'fun' run at work. They often think that everyone is as interested in the material aspects of life as they are.

Of course, every human being has a body, or else he would not be a human. What my vision revealed is that people must recognize which dominance they are and try to stay in balance. If a Body Dominant individual, who is pushing the negative extreme end, begins to become hyper-critical of others, then that person should try to bring him/herself back into a more balanced position. The Body Dominant needs to realize that a tidy desk and a spotless kitchen floor is not everybody's priority.

I once had a colleague who was a neat freak. She would go on a rampage in our office, criticizing us all for our messy desks. To me, they were not particularly messy, but to her the whole situation was intolerable. She used to be overly critical of one desk in our office that had several years' worth of files on it. One day, she said to me, "Margot, aren't you appalled by so and so's desk? Don't you think that we all need to speak to this person and have it cleaned up?"

"No," I said. "It really does not bother me at all." She could not believe that I was not irritated like she was about it. But, I am not Body Dominant. Someone else's desk really does not bother me. I remember looking at her one day thinking, "You are going to get sick one of these days because you are so anal about cleanliness." Unfortunately, soon after this incident, my colleague was diagnosed with colon cancer. I believe that there was a definite relationship between her Body Dominance imbalance and her disease.

Another woman I met was obsessed with the cleanliness of her home. If she came to my house, I felt I had to ensure that every speck of dust was taken care of, because if there were one flaw she would find it and draw my attention to it. In the case of the colleague at work who had the very messy desk, I was not bothered by comments about her desk. Even though I am Soul Dominant and am not as affected by my physical environment as Body Dominant people are, I am hurt when this woman criticizes my space, finding flaws in my housekeeping. Chores are not my highest priority. As a result, I do not invite her over very often; matter of fact, very few people do. She generally ends up sitting in her immaculate condominium all by herself.

I have seen people who notice every single flaw on their skin, every mark, red vein and freckle. They weigh themselves regularly and calculate grams of fat. Sometimes women look like they are wearing a mask of make-up and a wig, because they have spent so much time on their appearance, ensuring everything is in its place. The part that intrigues me is that these people are very often gorgeous, but they do not see themselves that way.

The vision told me that each personality dominance responds to stress differently and we all try to gain power in the most familiar way. A stressed out Body Dominant person naturally expresses stress through the Body Aspect. A Body Dominant might go shopping and spend way too much money, they may starve themselves to gain control over their body, or they might act like a storm blowing through the house, ordering anyone in their way to clean up. A Body Dominant might start picking away at his/her spouse, pointing out imperfections that do not exist in their mate, cutting them down without just cause. This behavior is simply the Body Dominant's way of gaining control in what appears to be an out of control situation. But, the problem, or the source of his frustration is not the issue itself; it is the Body Dominant's lack of perceived power.

Perhaps something happened at work and this is the Body Dominant's way of lashing out in a fashion related to his dominance. That is why it is so important for people to recognize if they are Body Dominant and to recognize if they are in a close relationship with a Body Dominant individual. Just because the Body Dominant person thinks that we need to improve our personal appearance does not mean that there is anything wrong with us. The physical aspect of life is the lens that they look through. They have a heightened sensitivity to their physical environment and, as a result, they tend to notice flaws wherever they look. When out of balance, Body Dominants can become unjustifiably critical. Just because a Body Dominant person thinks that our house is a mess because we did not make our bed this morning, or we left a coffee cup in the sink, does not mean that we are slobs. We all need to realize when we, or the Body Dominant people we live or work with, become out of balance. It is then that we can lighten up a little bit. I have included a chart to highlight the characteristics of the out of balance Body Dominant.

Stressed-Out Body Dominance

- Becomes obsessed by flaws they perceive about their bodies, so resorts to excessive waxing, tweezing, hair treatments, fingernail applications

- Decides to diet, even when not necessary -may become bulimic or anorexic

- Keeps the house absolutely immaculate, and practically untouchable; will ensure the kitchen tap, for example, is shiny before leaving the house

- Decides to redecorate, at great expense, because the house is not perfect

- Will spend hours each day in the garden, not out of enjoyment, but to be sure that all edges are straight and all weeds are pulled

- Complains about other's yards, homes, desks, offices that do not meet their standard of organization and cleanliness, not recognizing they are becoming overly conscious of their environment because they are stressed

- Begins to lose friends by being too critical

Parenting Implications

For those of you readers who are parents, let's go back to the day you waited breathlessly as the doctor examined your new baby's body? Ten fingers, ten toes, two legs, two arms, and so on. The doctor checked the baby's coloring, to ensure that he/she was getting enough oxygen. Your baby was measured and weighed and soon after, the doctor came to your bedside to give you the report. The Body Aspect features in our lives right from birth.

There are a myriad of books on the market that teach new parents about child development, like Johnson and Johnson's or Dr. Spock. These books outline the milestones of child physical and intellectual development, but always caution that parents must recognize that all children are different. Nevertheless, as new parents, we often feel more secure knowing that our children are reaching the milestones at the appropriate ages. Johnson's parenting book, *Your Baby from 6 to 12 months: A Step-by-Step Guide for Parents,*[15] offers the following milestone objectives: at four months, babies should be starting solid foods in the form of pablum, by six months, bottom teeth should be emerging and your baby should be sleeping through the night, by twelve months, your baby should be able to sit unsupported, crawl, pull him/herself up to standing position, cruise and hold onto furniture, stand momentarily without support and maybe walk two or three steps on her own. At that stage, your child should be able to bang two blocks together, feed him/herself finger foods, put objects in a container, point and hold a tiny object between forefinger and thumb. By thirteen months, your baby should be uttering understandable words, babble, respond to simple commands, recognize her name and other familiar words, use gestures like shaking her head for "no" and imitate words.

Some intellectual milestones that should be reached by twelve months are: finding hidden objects easily, exploring objects in different ways – banging, throwing, or dropping, understanding cause and effect – shake a rattle, it makes a noise. At this stage, your baby should be able to drink from a cup, brush her hair and listen to the telephone.

Now that you have been reminded of those milestones, do you remember the parents who gathered around talking about how their children have surpassed the milestones much earlier than other 'normal' children? You see a baby walking at nine months old while you were the parent fretting because your child was seventeen months old and still only crawling. Take heart. It is very possible that your child is simply not a Body Dominant. He/She may be more Mind Dominant, Spirit Dominant, or Soul Dominant.

What we want to achieve in our lives and the lives of our children is balance between the four aspects, Body, Mind, Spirit and Soul. However, the problem is that our medical or education professions have not created a milestone chart for spirit or soul development. The point is to recognize each of the different aspects we are born into and honor and respect the varying degrees and levels of each person's development.

For example, Mara had two children, Evan and Sarah, born two years apart. Evan refused from day one to latch onto Mara's breast for feeding. He would not try new foods. As he got older, he could not stand having to play soccer with all of the other neighborhood kids and preferred a quiet routine. Mara finally gave up enrolling him in sports programs and, instead, encouraged his more creative side. His sister, Sarah on the other hand, latched onto her mother's breast in the delivery room, after making immediate eye contact with her Mom. At four months, when she was fed pablum for the first time, Sarah grabbed the spoon from Mara and began feeding herself. At nine months, Mara found Sarah climbing the curtains and hanging from the top of the curtain rod. Sarah loved sports and joined every school team from soccer, basketball, track, to wrestling.

It turned out that Evan was born Spirit Dominant, while Sarah who demonstrated high Body Dominant characteristics as a baby, turned out to be Mind Dominant. As a toddler, she always pulled out the scruffiest, stained shirt and pants to wear. She would never let her mother put a bow in her hair, or dress her in a girly outfit, with tights and shiny shoes. She would struggle and rip them all off. She preferred puzzles and liked to fix objects around the house. In fact, at age four, she regularly fixed minor appliances. Her older brother Evan had few Body Dominant traits. He was comfortable wearing the same shirt every day and gave his personal appearance very little notice. He could only socialize with friends for a short time and then he would retreat to his own space and his own 'daydreams'.

Body Dominant parents may not understand a Mind or Spirit Dominant child who does not thrive in sports activities, who keeps a disorganized binder that is stuffed full of papers, or who comes out of his room with different colored socks on and a rumpled shirt. That is not to say that Mind, Spirit, or Soul Dominant children do not need to attend to their Body Aspect by doing physical exercise, or wearing decent clothes. All that I am saying is that they may need to be taught the value of these traits. Good grooming habits do not necessarily come naturally to all children. As far as physical fitness goes, they may need to engage in sports like long distance running, rowing, or hiking where the sport is more individual; a sport they can engage in while letting their mind or spirit wander. They generally do not fare as well in the higher contact sports like soccer or football.

Overall Implications

The Body Dominant person is typically very accomplished in interacting with his or her environment. This is not the case for all people. You will find that Mind, Spirit and Soul Dominant people are not quite as adept at, nor do they take as much pleasure in, enjoying the physical, sensual human experience. The sad part is that these people often do not even realize how pleasurable the human experience can actually be. This is something that I have learned over the last four years since this vision came to me, that time in this physical body is over like the flash of a firefly.

Body Dominant people, might consider, for their own personal evolution, to become more acquainted with their other four dimensions, including their God Aspect.

CHAPTER NINE

Mind Dominance

Slowly the thinker went on his way and asked himself: "What is it that you wanted to learn from teachings and teachers, and although they taught you much, what was it they could not teach you?" And he thought: "It was the Self, the character and nature of which I wished to learn."[16]

Herman Hesse (1877 – 1962) in *Siddhartha*

꒥

Siddhartha, in Herman Hesse's book by the same name, embarks on a journey to discover the meaning of life, much like Santiago did in *The Alchemist*. He begins as a thinker, reasoning through observations, cause and effect relationships and the examples set by teachers. Finally, he realizes that he cannot find the meaning of life by looking outside himself. He must search within.

Mind Dominant people are the thinkers. Rather than having a physical relationship with the environment, Mind Dominant people interact with the world in a very intellectual manner. Their knowledge comes from what they perceive through their five senses. While a Body Dominant person will enjoy the subtle mixture of sweet and sour in a sauce and the textures of mixed greens of a salad, a Mind Dominant person would want to find out the recipe's exact proportions of ingredients and the system for assembling the dish. A Body Dominant person thrives on the fast moving plays of basketball, reaching through other players, grasping the ball away from a competitor and dribbling the ball through the maze of players, for the perfect lay-up. The Mind Dominant person thrives on the statistics and game strategy. Mind Dominant people prefer to observe and develop systems from what they interpret, while a Body Dominant wants to actually feel, taste, touch, smell and hear.

I always think of the high school science experiment as a great example of how the Mind Dominant person finds his or her truth. First there is the hypothesis, then the method, followed by the observations (as set out by the five senses), and lastly the conclusion. Mind Dominant people follow logic, not intuition. They enjoy reading newspapers, watching the news, or reading non-fiction materials. Knowledge for them must be proven, based on empirical evidence. Unlike the Body Dominant, they may not love to shop or decorate their homes, create savory meals, or be the star on the basketball team.

Instead, Mind Dominant people enjoy fields such as engineering, accounting and science…any field where they can logically, using their five senses, understand the world around them. To the extreme, they are the stereotypical 'nerds', who have a pocket stuffed full of pens and wear pants that show the black socks underneath. Of course, Mind Dominant people are still good looking, groom themselves and play sports. It is just that Mind Dominant people do not care as much about their wardrobe, or their hairstyle, as a Body Dominant person does.

My colleague who helps me out with computer problems is in this group. Whenever I have a printing problem and ask him for help, he holds the mouse, darting around the screen, showing me the amazing capabilities of this brilliant invention. His eyes are blazing with excitement, while mine are glazed over and exasperated. I finally say, "But, I just want to print." He is Mind Dominant and, therefore, derives enormous pleasure from seeking out the answers to crossword puzzles, determining the winning move in chess games, calculating the solutions to math problems and tracking the stock market.

When my eldest son was in grade three, he would arrive home from school every Monday with a math 'problem of the week' to solve. To me, the problem seemed like gobbledy-gook. There never seemed to be enough information to solve it. Nevertheless, I would sit down with him and we would try to make some sense of the problem. One evening, however, panic ensued. We had worked on the problem for over half an hour, trying numbers on to see if they would work. Defeated, I finally blurted out, "Eric, I'm sorry, but this problem must have been designed by someone who loves solving riddles. I don't. I have things to do. I can't waste any more time on this."

Ashamed of myself, I made an appointment with his teacher to find out if these problems were created out of a math theme that Eric was taught in class and was then expected to apply at home. "Oh, no," she said, "These problems are designed so that children can have a sense of fun, trying new numbers on until they finally find the solution. Half an hour is not really that much time. That is why they are given a whole week to complete the problem. They just keep trying on systems until they find one that works. The children will feel a great sense of accomplishment and excitement having solved the puzzle."

Now, that sounds great in theory, but there was absolutely no excitement at our kitchen table - only frustration, tears and a sense of futility. We both realized that our brains were not designed to understand math. My son is eighteen years old now and I am forty-six. Math is still beyond our intellectual reach and has yet to bring us any sort of joy or sense of accomplishment. I really thought that having completed three university degrees, I would be able to solve a grade three math 'problem of the week' a little easier.

The fact is that some people love these sorts of puzzles and I appreciate these people who view the world through their intellect - the engineers who designed the bridge I travel over every morning to work, the scientists who invented the heart bypass surgery that saved my father's life and my accountant who makes sure that I get the best mortgage rate, and ensures that my tax returns save me the most amount of money and are submitted on time.

I have created a character trait list to highlight the Mind Dominant individual.

Mind Dominant Characteristics

- May have begun reading at an early age, loved Lego and puzzles, learned times tables early

- Enjoys understanding how objects operate, likes computers, DVD's, engines, tools and will read the manuals

- May become so absorbed in projects that they lose track of time and can be chronically late

- Less concerned about personal appearance, so wears mismatched or dated clothing, hair may appear scruffy, body may be out of shape because physical fitness and nutrition are not high priority

- Desk and office may be piled high with papers, books, half-eaten snacks and moldy coffee cups, but knows exactly where all important papers have been placed

The Negative Side of the Mind Dominant

Sometimes extremely high Mind Dominant people need to be reminded to take a shower, or cut their hair, or have it pointed out that their shirt does not match their tie and neither shirt nor tie matches their pants. Mind Dominant people are so absorbed by their intellectual pursuits that their Body Aspect takes a lesser importance. Their office or apartment may have stacks of papers everywhere, their bicycle and bench press are in the living room, for the beauty of a Mind Dominant's space is not as important as it would be to a Body Dominant individual.

A Mind Dominant person may become a workaholic, criticizing others for not remaining at work until the wee hours of the morning to finish a project, not realizing that co-workers may not be as enthusiastic about figuring out the solution to the puzzle or project. Mind Dominant's may be overcritical of other people's intelligence and lose friends over sarcastic comments. They might become so absorbed in their work that their family suffers from neglect.

I have created a list of stressed out Mind Dominant characteristics.

Stressed Out Mind Dominant

- Becomes a workaholic, staying up late to finish projects

- Desk and office becomes overwhelmingly disorganized and may begin to smell
- Insomnia sets in because mind will not shut off
- May resort to alcohol or drugs to alleviate stress
- Physical fitness routine is discontinued because of 'lack of time'
- Nutrition breaks down in favor of fast food
- Starts to push others to work harder, failing to recognize that others are not stressed and have healthier priorities such as family, health and recreation
- Becomes hyper critical and may see others as inferior, incompetent, or a "waste of skin"
- Begins to lose friends, colleagues, or family because of a hard-driving attitude

A really good example of a Mind Dominant character, in fictional lore, is Charles Dicken's, Ebenezer Scrooge. Scrooge was totally focused on making money, which he rarely spent because he was not Body Dominant and did not care for beautiful things. He ate gruel because the taste of food was not a priority. He worked long hours, even into Christmas Eve and expected his assistant, Bob Cratchett, to do the same. Luckily for Scrooge, the ghosts of Christmas Past, Present, and Future visited upon him and taught him that there was more to life than making money and working long hours to do it. Scrooge learned to open his heart to others and to enjoy a good meal. He, ultimately, began to treat himself and others better. This brought him happiness.

Body/Mind Balance

It is obvious, of course, that everyone has a mind and a body. We access both throughout our day. We also have a left hand and a right hand. If we are right handed, it does not mean that our left hand dangles by our side, limp and useless. Our left hand supports our right hand. The vision simply told me to understand that some people favor, or value, one aspect over the other and that they do this quite unconsciously. They cannot understand why more people are not like them.

A balance between the Body and the Mind Aspects is critical in many career choices. For example, an elite basketball player has to be intelligent; he has to have a very active Mind Aspect, or else he would not be able to quickly set up the best play at the best time. He has chosen a very physical way of interacting with the world, rather than a typical 'mind' way, like engineering. The basketball player needs the physical sensation of moving the ball around the court, pushing the body to the limit and interacting closely with other players on the floor. He thrives on the sensations basketball gives him.

Some people's minds seem to be more adept at solving problems than others. They can sit for hours on end, working out a problem on the computer. To stay in balance though, a Mind Dominant person must recognize that personal hygiene is important, as is exercise and nutrition.

A friend of mine, who was Mind Dominant, came over for a drink one day and opened my fridge. He quickly began to organize my fridge with all of the bottles lined up in order of height and contents. Any duplicate products were poured into each other and the bottles were recycled. As a Mind Dominant individual, this friend thrived on business ventures, making the deals, negotiating, putting all his 'ducks in a row'. He needed to put my fridge in a system. I told him that my fridge was not such a big deal to me. Was it mere coincidence that he was on anti-depressants, not me? His overwhelming need to organize everyone had left him feeling empty and, in turn, he became clinically depressed.

My vision told me that we should be much more conscious of our dominance so that we can maintain a sense of joy in our lives. If we become too dominant in one aspect, it can interfere with our joy factor.

Parenting Implications

Parenting and child-rearing books outline, in detail, the intellectual milestones of our children, just as they do for the physical. My recommendation is to recognize and understand the dominant aspect of your child and not to fret if your child is not talking at twelve months old. Einstein's language development proceeded at a much slower rate than other children in his class. In fact, according to Michael Gelb's research, one of Einstein's teachers believed that young Einstein would "never amount to anything."[17] Some people are more thinkers than talkers. Do not worry if your friend's baby is walking at nine months and yours is still sitting, taking apart your pots and pans drawer. Observe your child to see if you can recognize which dominance he or she is.

Being a high school teacher, I have an endless stream of grade twelve students worried about disappointing their parents. They want to please their parents, but at the same time want to pursue a career that will bring them meaning and joy. Some Mind Dominant parents insist their child become a doctor, lawyer, or engineer, as if these careers are the only valuable ones. The student sitting in front of me may only have a 60% average and will most likely not even go to university, let alone become a doctor. This student may have a desire to become a massage therapist instead. But, the Mind Dominant parent does not value this Body Dominant characteristic and, therefore, does not value their offspring's choice of career. This kind of misunderstanding can very well drive parent and child apart. I guess this dilemma follows the old cliché of stuffing a square peg through a round hole. We, as parents, must somehow value the world view that Body, Mind and Spirit Dominant children hold. We must realize that our priorities may not be their priorities. This holds true for all of the people in our lives – parents, siblings, employees, employers, and so on.

My hope is that people will see themselves in the model that I am creating so that they can recognize when they are stressed out or neglecting an aspect of themselves.

CHAPTER TEN

Spirit Dominance

I wasn't certain myself, I was thinking of all the schemes he'd had, the ones that couldn't possibly have worked, the unreal solutions to which he'd clung because there were not others, the brave and useless strokes of fantasy against a depression that was both the world's and his own.

"I don't know," I said. "I just think things were always more difficult for him than he let on, that's all. Remember that letter?"

"Yes."

"Well – what it said was that they could force his body to march and even to kill, but what they didn't know was that he'd fooled them. He didn't live inside it any more."

"Oh, Vanessa –" my mother said. "You must have suspected right then."

"Yes, but –"

I could not go on, could not say that the letter seemed only the final heartbreaking extension of that way he'd always had of distancing himself from the absolute unbearability of the battle.[18]

Margaret Laurence (1926 –1987) in the short story *Horses of the Night*

꙰

Laurence, in her book *Horses of the Night*, writes of Chris, a young man who lives with such a vibrant optimism about life. He is alive with passion and dreams for his future, despite the criticism from his family at the unrealistic nature of his plans. They laugh at him and continuously remind him of how futile his ambitions are. Eventually, Chris goes to war and returns a broken man left to wither away in a mental institution. His family views him despairingly, but Chris has a secret. His body is in the mental institution, but his spirit is somewhere else, realizing his passions and dreams.

When I talk about Spirit Dominant people, many Mind Dominant individuals assume that Spirit Dominance is peaceful and easy. For many Spirit Dominant people, taking on a human body and living on Earth is far from easy. For some it is an unbearable battle.

I do not have any problem convincing people that they have a body and a mind. Our society is even designed to serve the needs of the body and mind. Most people grasp the idea that they can be Body Dominant or Mind Dominant. However, many people are sketchy about the idea that we have a Spirit Aspect, that there is a spirit looking out through our eyes, that the spirit has capabilities all of its own, just as the body and mind do. I was surprised and intrigued at finding out that a person can be Spirit Dominant. I was even more intrigued by the revelation that a person could be Spirit Dominant and not know it. This part of the vision came as a complete surprise.

A Spirit Dominant person perceives his or her environment predominantly through the Spirit Aspect. I am talking about the Spirit Aspect that looks just like you, the part of you that will go to the spiritual dimension when your body dies. However, many Spirit Dominant people do not realize that their Spirit Aspect is struggling to make sense of the physical, tangible world. The Spirit Aspect longs for the ideal, peaceful, euphoric realm of unconditional love. But it looks out through eyes that see consumerism, power struggles, jealousies and endless, incessant hustle and bustle.

The Spirit Aspect has the capability to reach into the spiritual dimension to pull down wonderful truths. However, finding the proper words, words that feel like heavy, limiting and confining boxes to the Spirit Dominant person, can cause intense internal struggle. Experiencing the insight is often a euphoric experience, but conveying the idea to a Mind Dominant person, who views the world through the five senses, can seem futile. Being Spirit Dominant might lead to tremendous highs, but sadly it can also lead to miserable lows.

There are countless books on the market today, teaching people how to become more spiritual. In our society, there are thousands of people embarking on spiritual journeys. But for those of us born Spirit Dominant, life is not so easy. Spirit Dominant people very often look at the world and wonder what it is coming to. Why are people becoming workaholics and neglecting their families? For what? Money? Why are people ripping up the beautiful cliff sides to put in monstrous houses? Why are there homeless people laying in the shadows of our downtown alleyways?

We live in a society that values the Body and Mind Aspects. The childhood development books outline the milestones for physical and intellectual development, but they do not even recognize that there is a spirit development as well. For those of us who are Spirit Dominant, we need to learn how to become more body and mind conscious. We need a mentor to teach us how to preserve our natural joy while learning to become more human.

The Positive Side of Spirit Dominant

A Spirit Dominant child often has sparkly, compassionate eyes. He is the one who reaches up and strokes your head when you are having a stressful day. She empathizes with the sick and the unfortunate. These children find the wounded bird in the backyard and bring the lonely child home from school. They seem to know what you are thinking and try to help before you have even asked. They are idealists and try to preserve the very best of humanity. You will find them organizing a charity or a benefit of some kind to help others. They seem wise beyond their years, old souls.

Spirit Dominant people tend to need time for solitude, time to escape the prison of the body and let their spirit soar. High Spirit Dominant people, like myself, can connect with a spiritual dimension at will. Many Spirit Dominant people have, in their 'daydream' state, conceived of some of the world's best inventions, works of art, or theories. Spirit Dominant people are the visionaries. They see beyond the five senses. Their awareness transcends the tangible and they can view what many cannot. This can be confusing because intuition is not highly regarded in our society. They are afraid of being labeled 'mentally ill.' They can see the extraordinary in the ordinary, but often lack the Body Dominant strength and the Mind Dominant organization skills to put their insight into action.

Since their insight often comes as a blast of complete 'knowingness', Spirit Dominant people often have difficulty finishing projects because the arduous task of organizing information for Body/Mind Dominant people is time consuming. Spirit Dominant people tend to be able to 'just know' how things work, while Body/Mind people need all of the details organized for them. Many Spirit Dominant people cannot bother to do the fiddly paperwork to get their visions to the forefront of society's consciousness. To Body/Mind individuals, the Spirit Dominant person may appear as an underachieving dreamer. I have outlined below some of the characteristics of the Spirit Dominant individual.

Spirit Dominant Characteristics

- Idealist who believes that the intangibles of life, like love, peace, friendship, joy, compassion are the most important achievements

- Requires some solitary time each day and can become overwhelmed in a noisy and busy environment

- Needs time to daydream and fantasize

- Enjoys talks on philosophical matters such as why are we here and where are we going, alternate realities and God, not small talk

- Believes more in knowledge gained from personal experience than scientific theory

- Has energetic, sparkly eyes

- Gets lost easily or misplaces objects when caught between the spirit world and the physical world

- Thrives in and enjoys natural settings that are quiet and have water, rather than urban areas

- Has definite passions

If we think back to the football game analogy, there was a point when our spirits were taken away from the security of the bench and sent into the rough and tumble game of human life. I found out, in my vision, that not everyone was as willing as the next to take on the human form. Some Spirit Dominant children prefer to sit on the bench and not engage fully in the game of life. Some Spirit Dominant babies are not ready to adjust to the human form. Body Dominant people thrive in their bodies. They love the sensual experience. In contrast, Spirit Dominant people can feel imprisoned by the human body and long to return to the unconditional love and peacefulness of 'heavenly life'. The problem is that Spirit Dominant people, who often think in pure thought rather than words, find it difficult to convey their feelings of loneliness to others and as a result live a somewhat isolated lifestyle.

The Negative Side of the Spirit Dominant

As I said before, our society is designed to embrace the Body/Mind Aspects. Our school system is set up to assist children in developing their bodies in gym class, and their minds in Science, Math, English and Social Studies. The Spirit Aspect, in my experience of twenty-three years, is not only ignored in public education, but consciously left out of the curriculum.

I recognize that religious organizations can greatly benefit the developing spirit. But, some people treat religious doctrine from a Mind Dominant lens, not leaving any room for people to explore their own experiences of contacting God, or talking to spirits. Some people accept their religion through a Body Dominance in that they feel a physical security offered by their religious beliefs. When I am talking about educating the spirit, I am talking about nurturing children in their own understanding of spirit. We neglect this discussion in education, for fear of treading on people's religious beliefs. I believe that educators are unsure of how to deal with spirit and, therefore, leave this to religious leaders.

Children's spirits have their own experiences, just as the body and mind do. There are children who see spirits, hear voices, have premonitions and have out of body experiences. But researchers such as Alistair Hardy[19], David Hay and Rebecca Nye[20], have found that children rarely tell anyone about what they see, especially not their parents. As these children grow into adults, some have developed their Mind and Body Aspects and consciously repress their Spirit Aspect just so that they can fit in. What I have found in some of my adolescent students is that they are unconscious of their Spirit Aspect. They do not realize that they have a spirit that looks out through their eyes. They are unaware that this spirit can get stuck in time and place, or on a person. What some of my students are aware of is a profound sense of loneliness. They will retreat into their spiritual dimension far too often by daydreaming, sleeping far too long, or simply disengaging with family and school.

Parents and teachers often negatively react to the perceived disengagement of their child or student. They become frustrated because they cannot understand why the teen is so unmotivated, why he does not do anything, why he would prefer to isolate himself from the rest of the world by sleeping away the day, or escaping in alcohol or drugs. Spirit Dominant teens are actually retreating to a spiritual world, complete with family and friends. A mind/body parent or teacher only sees an immobile mind and body before them, but there is a question to ask that likely will make all the difference.

I met a boy recently who was virtually invisible in my classroom. He rarely completed an assignment and never spoke a word. One lunch hour, I heard a knock at my classroom door, and there he was. "Can I talk to you?" he asked. He went on to tell me that he could not participate in my class because he was too shy. I had already determined that he was a stressed out Spirit Dominant. He kept himself almost invisible, never engaged in any class activities and lived in a world of his own. The question I asked was, "Your body is in class, but the real you isn't. Where does the real you go when the rest of us are working on the class material?" His eyes had more sparkle in them after that question than I had seen all semester. Usually, he had what I call 'dead eyes', eyes without any spirit looking out of them. He looked straight into my eyes for the first time and, with a grin, he said that he goes to a special place. He went on to say that his mother died when he was six years old and he goes to a place where he can be with his mother.

He also said that there is a little girl in that place too, a little girl that he is meant to adopt when he is older.

His story did not surprise me at all. I have heard a few other versions since I started asking that question. One student told me that he goes to a skateboard park with his friends. I asked him if they were friends from here, or from over there, referring to the spiritual dimension. "From over there," was his reply. I asked another boy where he goes when he gets sick of all of us. He grinned and said, "I go to a place that tells me about parallel universes, where energy merges, you know... quantum physics." Another boy hiked through the mountains, went kayaking and designed and built a log cabin.

The first boy, the one that loved to spend time with his mother, said that he found it too difficult to do school work, that he would much rather stay with his mother. He said that living in this world was not that much fun. It made perfect sense to him, however, that he should start learning to have fun. He could grasp the idea that he could take more enjoyment in eating food, doing exercise, and reading and writing about his experiences. He is at least trying to honor his other aspects now and I continue encouraging him to find pleasure in his human experience.

Spirit Dominant people tend to enjoy their own company more than the company of others and will retreat to a quiet place when their environment becomes overwhelmingly busy and noisy. However, they typically have many projects on the go, some in their minds and some tangible ones and they escape into them. They may become lost in books for hours at a time, or in a more creative project like writing, art, gardening, photography, or woodworking, to name just a few examples. They tend to enjoy working in solitude, where they can let their spirits roam without the constant noise and interruption of human life.

The boy who liked hiking and kayaking decided to take kayaking courses and worked up in northern British Columbia for the summer as an archeologist's assistant. He hiked into the remote parts of the forests in search of native artifacts. He loved it. To help Spirit Dominant people, we must remember that their interior world is real to them and that it is possible to turn their physical, tangible and intellectual existence into a replica of what is in their interior world.

To be honest, before I had this vision I had kind of written off these types of students as unreachable. It never occurred to me that they had a vibrant interior world. It never occurred to me that they had a need to be invisible and that this was a protective device. Being invisible allowed them to stay under the radar of probing Mind/Body eyes. If your eyes scan a room, there are some people that you just might skip over, as if they are not even really there.

As a high school teacher, I am now able to see from the very first day which students are the very physical Body Dominant ones, the intellectual Mind Dominant students and the quiet, unassuming Spirit Dominant individuals. As my students enter the classroom, I am now more conscious about recognizing these three types of people. Some students are very physical. They tend to be highly visible, perhaps loud and chatty, fashionable, athletic and good looking and scout out the most comfortable chair and desk in the room. The intellectual Mind Dominant students, although good looking, may not give their appearance and fashion sense the same amount of attention as the physical students. The Spirit Dominant students glide in, as if ghosts, and quietly take their seats. They very often prefer if the teacher took no notice of them whatsoever and sometimes even dress in baggy clothing, wearing hats or hoodies to make themselves even less visible. Out comes the Ipod and they retreat into their music.

Some Spirit Dominant people need to retreat to their bedrooms as much as they can to escape the human experience. As a society, I think that we assume that everyone who is born is ready to take on the human form, ready to breathe, walk, talk and eat. We assume that all children are naturally excited to play sports, ride a bike and climb trees. We assume that by age five, children cannot wait to leave home, start school, learn to read, write and do arithmetic. Is it not normal for all children to want to build a circle of friends, go to summer camps and try adventurous skills?

If you have had a child who seemed resistant as a baby, would not eat, would not sleep, would not try anything new, then you know that not all children embrace what life has to offer. If you had a child who had temper tantrums, disrupted the routines of your family, seemed completely unhappy in his own skin, then you know that not all children desire to be here on Earth. If you had a child who retreated to his bedroom, played with an imaginary friend, arrived with 'wise beyond his years' ideas, seemed to understand what you were feeling just by looking at you, then you may very well have had the challenging task of raising a Spirit Dominant child. Below, I have listed some characteristics of the stressed out Spirit Dominant person.

Stressed Out Spirit Dominant

- Resorts to daydreaming, or excessive sleeping, to avoid the reality that everything is not ideal

- Becomes more solitary and isolated

- Finds daily activities too noisy and overwhelming

- House and office become messy and disorganized

- Lacks motivation or desire to go out into the world

- Practically becomes invisible

- Eyes lose their sparkle

- May use drugs or alcohol to recapture the feeling of being in a state of the ideal, rather than the pain of coping with 'reality'

- May mutilate themselves or have thoughts of suicide because they want to shed their human form and go into spirit where they feel safe

- May hear condemning voices, or have disturbing visions that point out inadequacies

- Friends and family may fear a nervous breakdown or mental illness has set in

Parenting Implications

When I discovered the Body, Mind, Spirit, Soul Dominance Theory, I believed that I was Spirit Dominant and that I needed to learn how to be a better human being, how to derive more pleasure from the human experience and how to teach other Spirit Dominant individuals to do the same. Ever since I was a preschooler, I knew that there was more to the human being than just a body and a mind, but in a society that prizes physical and intellectual achievements, Spirit Dominant children can feel more and more isolated.

Some Spirit Dominant people appear lazy and argumentative, when in reality they are struggling with the daily demands of human life. It had never occurred to me before that perhaps some people do not really want to be humans, that they never asked to be born, that they have difficulty adjusting to the physical and intellectual demands of life on Earth. While other children thrive on the athletic field, Spirit Dominant children may retreat and avoid the rough play of sports. Just as I become anxious when I am forced to deal with math, some people become anxious when they must meet deadlines at school or work, face confrontational relationships, or try something new, even if it is a delicious food. Some people resist and would much rather stay sheltered in a comfort zone of their own making.

Spirit Dominant children born to Body/Mind Dominant parents can suffer in silence, while their parents are running around trying to sign them up for more sports activities or more remedial courses, without realizing what the real problem might be. As teens, these Spirit Dominant individuals, may opt out of this human experience and retreat into the spiritual realm by sleeping a lot, or 'daydreaming', or living in the peacefulness of the country. They may resort to alcohol and drugs to escape the misery they feel in their human experience. Some resort to cutting themselves, actually trying to destroy their bodies while others go to the extreme of attempting suicide because they just want to go 'home'. They do not want a human experience. They recognize, consciously or unconsciously, that they have a spirit that lives inside the body and that this spirit simply longs for the peaceful, quiet, complete unconditional love of the spirit world. In many of their activities,

Spirit Dominant people strive to recreate the tranquility of the spiritual dimension they knew before taking on the human form. Often, they become confused by the hustle and bustle of daily human affairs.

What I have found as a high school teacher is that my Spirit Dominant students often end up in the non-academic stream of education. They are put in basic level classes that will lead them to a high school diploma, but not to university. However, these Spirit Dominant students exhibit to me a brilliance of original thinking, or deep and troubling angst about being a human being. In my view, teachers must learn how to recognize the Spirit Dominant student and must have the teaching knowledge necessary to assist these students in fulfilling their brilliance. I have found that once my students learn that their angst stems from being Spirit Dominant and that their purpose in life is to come to terms with being a human - to start enjoying the taste of food, experimenting with fashion, going on hikes in the mountains, establishing friendships and enjoying human company, they immediately take on an attitude adjustment. The Spirit Dominant explanation makes sense to them.

A common story I hear from my grade twelve students is that they have a parent (often Mind Dominant) who expects them to become a doctor, lawyer, or engineer. They feel as though they are disappointing their parents, while at the same time they feel their parent does not value who they are. Spirit Dominant children may not necessarily want the outward appearance of success, like a title of doctor, or the luxury of a big house. Their parents sometimes cannot understand their decision to live a quiet, contemplative life. Some parents feel that their children are 'copping' out, that they are tragic underachievers. My suggestion is to empathize with them. Honor who they 'really' are, support and nurture and try to find ways to make their tangible, exterior lives match their vibrant interior worlds. Keep the sparkle in their eyes.

My goal now is to assist children and teens to learn to love being a human being, to value the experience and to use their spiritual insight to help our society evolve. At the same time, I hope to assist physical and intellectual people to access their spirit dimension, so that they can enjoy the peacefulness, creativity and wisdom it can offer. I created a list of what some characteristics would be for an individual who desires to live a balanced body, mind, spirit human experience.

Characteristics of a Balanced Body, Mind, Spirit

- Physically fit
- Showers every day, if possible, and wears appropriate, neat clothing
- Keeps a tidy home, yard and vehicle
- Engages in intellectual pursuits like reading, coursework, conversation
- Creates a life that fulfills passion
- Spends a portion of the day with others at work or home, but takes time out for solitary activities
- Takes trips to the country to rejuvenate
- Gets an adequate amount of sleep each day
- Creates a circle of friends that are meaningful and supportive of passions and the need to understand life's purpose
- Fulfills the requirements of mind activities like using a computer, filling in tax forms, or reading a map, rather than avoiding them
- Can recognize transitions between a body, a mind and a spirit activity

Overall Implications

I have finally figured out why some people are naturally able to snap a tennis ball across a net, run a ten kilometer race with minimal training, or fare pretty well in the company golf tournament even though they rarely swing a club. I have also found out why others bump into everyone else in a fitness class, zigging when others are zagging, moving left when the others are going right.

I figured out why some people's desks are immaculately organized right down to a paperclip container, scissor holder and color-coded file folders, while other desks are piled high with paper and books dripping onto the floor. Four years ago, I found out why some people love to be pampered with pedicures, facials and up-to-the-minute hairstyles. I figured out why they love the fine details of interior design and the subtle flavors of food and wine, activities that excite the five senses, taste, touch, sound, sight and smell. These are the very physical people who notice the fine details of their environment, the colors, the shapes, the temperature and the aromas.

I really enjoy being invited to dinner by these very energetic, physical people. The candles are lit, fresh flowers grace the kitchen island, gentle flavors of thyme and rosemary waft from the oven and the table is set with matching cutlery and dinner plates. At my house, namely the domain of a high Spirit Aspect, when the guests arrive I am still trying to find enough chairs to go around the dining room table; I am unwrapping cheese to put on a platter that probably has a chip out of it; I am hoping above all hopes that I put the meat in on time and that the gravy has some flavor to it. At least now, I know why I am like this.

CHAPTER ELEVEN

Soul Dominance

If I can stop one heart from breaking,
I shall not live in vain;
If I can ease one life the aching,
Or cool one pain,
Or help one lonely person
Into happiness again
I shall not live in vain.[21]

Emily Dickinson (1830 – 1885)

⸙

Emily Dickinson evokes the core sentiments of a Soul Dominant person. The focus of the Soul Dominant life is to fulfill a purpose, a purpose that serves the greatest good, not just individual pleasure. While a Mind Dominant entrepreneur may derive significant gratification from opening several businesses, from flower shops to burger franchises, a Soul Dominant lives with a fairly singular focus – a purpose to serve.

As I mentioned earlier, as the vision was unfolding for me that Friday afternoon four years ago, I struggled with the idea that I might be Soul Dominant. Our soul, I was told, is that part of us that anchors us on this earthly plane with a definitive purpose. During the vision, however, I would not allow myself to pursue the Soul Dominance aspect. I felt, for some reason, as though it were above me, as though I were not ready to know the full implications of Soul Dominance. What I am revealing here about Soul Dominance, I have discovered subsequent to the original vision.

The central idea to the Dominance Theory is that each of us has been born more developed in one of the four aspects – Body, Mind, Spirit, or Soul. The vision did not reveal that we could be God Dominant, even though we have a God Aspect. We all have a Soul Aspect, a divine purpose and a Soul Dominant person is one who is compelled or driven to fulfill this purpose.

The Positive Side of Soul Dominance

A Soul Dominant person recognizes from a very early age that he or she has a significant purpose to fulfill and is compelled to focus unlimited time, resources and energy to serve this purpose. My purpose to fulfill the role of teacher is my reason for being. From the time I started school, I studied my teachers in order to learn about the craft; I stayed home on the occasional Friday night as a teen-ager to study for a test because I knew that my marks had to be high in order to get into my university of choice; I could not fathom other professions, even though they would provide me with a grander lifestyle than a teacher's salary. Even now, I give up evenings and week-ends to complete all of the marking necessary to be ready for class.

Some of my family and friends do not understand why I have stayed at teaching for so long. Now that I am divorced, my teaching salary barely covers month-to-month bills. I have not had an adventurous holiday in twenty years and my clothes closet has about four outfits in it. Why do I stay at teaching? Because I am compelled! There is a driving force within me that keeps me motivated and excited with my life path as a teacher. I do not see a difference between when work ends and my life begins. Teaching is a way of life for me. It is not just a job. It is not just a career. It is my soul purpose. I am Soul Dominant because I am compelled to fulfill my purpose.

My nephew, Fraser MacDougall[22], is struggling right now to honor his purpose of creating music that speaks to socially conscious issues, especially preserving the Earth and preserving sacred relationships. He shares a tiny apartment with two roommates, works at a store during the day and scrapes every spare penny together to promote his music and message. In the notes at the back of this book, I have listed his website so that readers can access it and hear his music. At the moment, he is verging on being financially broke. I wrote him an email saying that for Soul Dominant people like ourselves, we sacrifice to bring our purpose to life.

I spent all last summer, eight to twelve hours a day, writing this book. My friends were playing tennis, going on holidays and lunching in local bistros. I sat in my basement, on a concrete floor, at a computer day in and day out. Why? Because I am compelled to get the message out about Body, Mind, Spirit and Soul Dominance. I am willing to sacrifice. I spent every other week-end during the fall and winter, rewriting and editing. I tried to encourage my nephew, but at the same time, I recognize that at times it is difficult to be so compelled to fulfill a purpose.

Soul Dominant people are willing to put up with criticism from others who do not understand their dedication to purpose. They are willing to sacrifice their Body Aspect needs like beautifully decorated homes, delicious foods, or spa treatments in order to fulfill their destiny. The difference between Soul Dominant people and Mind Dominant individuals is that the Soul Dominant person has a narrower focus than the Mind Dominant. The Soul Dominant focuses energy to achieve one single, solitary goal, like being a teacher. A Mind Dominant person likely has many irons in the fire, so to speak. He or she loves the puzzle, the intellectual challenge of a task, rather than the purpose. A Mind Dominant entrepreneur may build up a number of different businesses. If they fail, he or she might declare bankruptcy and move on to build up another business. Their principle joy comes from intellectually tracking the economic market and timing a new venture to bring in the greatest cash rewards. That is not to say that Mind Dominant people are not socially conscious. They are simply not as compelled or driven by a single, divine purpose like Soul Dominant people are. Soul Dominant people recognize that they are driven by a force outside of themselves, a divine force.

Below is a list of characteristics of Soul Dominant people.

Soul Dominant Characteristics

- Recognizes at an early age that there is a divine purpose

- Compelled to achieve purpose and not very interested in subjects unrelated to purpose
- Organizes life to achieve this divine purpose through education, travel, volunteer work, career choice for example
- Will self-educate, rather than attend Mind Dominant universities, in order to stay true to purpose
- Willing to sacrifice a physically and socially comfortable life in order to reach goals
- Thrives on the difficult and sometimes uncomfortable work needed to fulfill purpose
- May not take care of physical appearance
- Recognition for efforts not as important as achieving results
- Willing to be fired from job than compromise purpose
- Many are willing to die for beliefs and purpose

Soul Dominant individuals are anchored to Earth by a strong sense of divine purpose. They are willing to sacrifice creature comforts in order to make their vision come true. Canadian writer, Robertson Davies, created the perfect, exemplary Soul Dominant character in his book, *Fifth Business*.[23] Davies' main character, Dunstan, or Dunny as he is commonly called, is obsessed with researching Saints because when he was a child he believed that Mrs. Dempster, the preacher's wife, performed miracles on three separate occasions. Dunny spends the rest of his life researching and writing best selling books about Saints. His role as temporary Headmaster is challenged by his boyhood nemesis, Boy Staunton, who has become the director of the private school where Dunny teaches. The following excerpt portrays a vivid description of a Soul Dominant individual, namely Dunny.

"You are a fine teacher, [Boy Staunton says]. Everybody knows it. You are a great scholarship-getter, which is quite another thing. You have a reputation as an author. But there it is."

"There is what?" [replies Dunny]

"It's this saint business of yours. Of course your books are splendid. But if you were a father, would you want to send your son to school headed by a man who was an authority on saints? Even more, would you do it if you were a mother? Women hate anything that's uncanny about a man if they think of entrusting a son to him. Religion in the school is one thing; there is a well-understood place for religion in education. But not this misty world of wonder-workers and holy wizards and juiceless women. Saints aren't in the picture at all. Now I'm an old friend, but I am also Chairman of the Board, and I tell you it won't do."

"Are you kicking me out?"

"Certainly not! Don't be extreme. You surely understand that you are a tremendous addition to the school as a master – well-known writer on a difficult subject, translated into foreign languages, amusingly eccentric, and all that – but you would be a disaster as a peacetime Headmaster."

"Eccentric? Me!"

"Yes, you. Good God, don't you think the way you rootle in your ear with your little finger delights the boys? And the way you waggle your eyebrows – great wild things like moustaches, I don't know why you don't trim them – and those terrible Harris tweed suits you wear and never have pressed. And that disgusting trick of blowing your nose and looking into your handkerchief as if you expected to prophesy something from the mess. You look ten years older than your age. The day of comic eccentrics as Heads has gone. Parents nowadays want somebody more like themselves."

Dunny and Boy work out a deal in which Dunny can take six months off from teaching and Boy will explain that the reason Dunny will not accept the position of Headmaster is that his writing takes up much of his time. The truth that he is passed over because of his obsession with his research on Saints is not to be revealed to the parents. Boy asks Dunny what he is going to do with his six month vacation.

"I have long wanted to visit the great shrines of Latin America. I shall begin in Mexico, with the Shrine of the Virgin of Guadalupe."

"There you go, you see! You go right on with the one thing that really stood between you and a Headmaster's job."

"Certainly. You don't expect me to pay attention to the opinion of numbskulls like you and your Board and the parents of a few hundred cretinous boys, do you?"

Personally, Dunny makes me laugh. He does not care how he is perceived by society. In his typically Soul Dominant style he is determined to find out whether Mrs. Dempster is a saint. His life is consumed with a sense of purpose, regardless of society's view and the cost to his career. He even has the characteristic lack of appreciation for his personal grooming. Many people who are not as driven as Soul Dominant individuals cannot understand the total conviction to purpose these types exhibit.

The Negative Side of the Soul Dominant

There is a lot to be admired about Soul Dominant people. Dian Fossey, for example, dedicated her life to preserving gorillas in Africa. Terry Fox who attempted to run across Canada on one leg to raise money and awareness for cancer research underwent grueling pain to achieve his vision. Many Soul Dominant people have made their way into our history books because they have achieved enormous results in the face of enormous obstacles. Unfortunately, many Soul Dominant individuals have been diagnosed with some sort of mental illness because their single-minded focus and dedication to purpose is sometimes too overwhelming for them.

Joan of Arc (Jeanne), born in 1411 or 1412, is a famous Soul Dominant individual. As a young teen-ager, standing only 4'8" tall, Jeanne managed what would likely seem impossible for any other nineteen year old. She inspired her French countrymen to ensure that her king, Dauphin Charles, was crowned. Jeanne made no secret of the fact that she was directed by angels, and by Saints Michael, Catherine, and Margaret in her fight to bring France back to its glory.

In Jeanne's day, hearing voices and acting according to their instructions was not considered as abnormal as it is today. After many battles, where she donned men's clothes and armor, Jeanne was finally captured on May 23, 1430. On February 24, 1431, her trial began. Pickels, in her book Joan of Arc, transcribed Jeanne's responses to the judge assigned to her trial. "I was thirteen when I had a voice from God for my help and guidance," she said.[24] "The first time that I heard this voice, I was very much frightened. It was midday, in the summer, in my father's garden. I had not fasted the day before. I heard this voice to my right, toward the church. Rarely do I hear it without it being accompanied also by a light. This light comes from the same side as the voice. Generally it is a great light. Since I came into France, I have often heard this voice."[25]

Jeanne was compelled to follow her purpose as set out by her God and to follow the instructions of the voices. She said, "There is not a day when I do not hear this voice, and I have much need of it. But never have I asked of it recompense but the salvation of my soul."[26] Unfortunately, Jeanne succumbed and renounced her visions and voice because she was under the false impression that if she recanted her story, she would spend the rest of her days in a church prison rather than be sentenced to burning. In fact, she was tricked into making the false confession. With that, she was riddled with guilt, "To save my life," she said, "I betrayed Him and in so doing I damned myself! The Voices have since told me that I did a great evil in declaring that what I had done was wrong. All that I said and revoked that Thursday, I did for fear of the fire."[27] Fire was Jeanne's greatest fear and when she was finally led to the stake where she was to be burned she requested that someone give her a cross to look at during her torture. Her greatest passion, to serve her God and her purpose, ultimately led to her terrifying death.

Soul Dominant people can become consumed by their fundamental need to fulfill their purpose. They are single-minded in their urgent desire to please God. Four hundred and ninety years later, in 1920, the Catholic Church canonized Joan of Arc.

Vincent Van Gogh, the famous Dutch painter, was another Soul Dominant individual who died in an attempt to fulfill his destiny. Van Gogh, born on March 30, 1853, had an insatiable appetite for spiritual knowledge. He wanted to be closer to God, and would give up any sort of creature comfort in order to achieve his desire. He would beat his body with a stick and sleep in the cold, on the bare floor, because he could not understand his relationship with God. Greenberg and Jordan printed excerpts of Van Gogh's letters to his brother, Theo, in their book *Vincent Van Gogh: Portrait of an Artist.* "Such a man does not always know what he could do", he wrote, "but he instinctively feels, I am good for something, my life has a purpose after all...how could I be useful, of what service can I be?"[28] Van Gogh struggled every day with fulfilling his purpose.

Van Gogh's letters to his parents became crammed with religious meditations, which worried them. His father, a Lutheran Pastor, decided that the solution was to enroll Van Gogh in a proper religious study program. According to the records, Van Gogh could not pass the courses because he failed the Greek verb section. Van Gogh could not understand how Greek verbs were relevant to his desire to "give peace to poor creatures and reconcile them to their existence here on earth."[29] Van Gogh was not going to be prevented from fulfilling the role God chose for him and elected to enroll in an evangelical school. His father got reports that he was starving himself and sleeping on the floor, instead of his bed.

In the first sermon that Van Gogh ever presented, he referred to himself as feeling like a stranger on Earth. That is a very typical sentiment of those who are Spirit Dominant and Soul Dominant. When Van Gogh's father discovered his son's desire to serve God, he enrolled Van Gogh in a seminary to learn more about the Bible and the Christian faith. Van Gogh did not fare well, as he soon recognized the hypocrisy of some of his instructors. They did not always espouse the kinds of virtues that Van Gogh believed those serving God should have. One example was the time there was a deadly mine explosion. Men were strewn about, many left for dead. With tremendous compassion, Van Gogh went to his room, tore up all of his clothes and bed linens, grabbed a jug of olive oil and began to tend the injured. He cleansed the wounds and dressed them. The preachers declared that Van Gogh was behaving like a lunatic, thinking that he could somehow save these men.

Van Gogh steadfastly believed in God and wrote, "I always think that the best way to know God is to love many things. Love a friend, a wife, something – whatever you like – you will be on your way knowing more about Him."[30] In a desperate attempt to prevent his friend and fellow artist, Gauguin, from leaving Arle, Van Gogh sliced off his ear with a razor. He did not remember doing this, but afterward Harris, in the book, *Masterworks: Van Gogh*, noted that he had written, "It was when I was in just such deep misery that I felt my energies revive and I said to myself: In spite of everything I shall rise again; I will take up my pencil, which I have forsaken in my great discouragement and I will go on with my drawing. And from that moment everything has seemed transformed for me; and now I have started and my pencil has become a little more docile with every day."[31]

The human experience can be very painful to Soul Dominant people. Their purpose can feel like both their greatest joy and their greatest misery. They can feel such elation, yet believe that they are never good enough. They can feel miserable because they do not perceive themselves as worthy.

My initial understanding of Van Gogh was that he was insane, having cut off his ear. As I researched this Soul Dominant person, I soon discovered that he wrestled on a daily basis with his path in life, his purpose, his connection to God. Van Gogh wrote to his brother upon the birth of his nephew, "I should like him to have a soul less unquiet than mine, which is foundering."[32] Sadly, Van Gogh's overwhelming desire to fulfill his purpose became too great and he committed suicide. Theo, his brother, wrote, "Life was a burden to [Vincent]; but now, as often happens, everyone is in praise of his talents."[33] For many Soul Dominant people, who struggle with their visions and their purpose in life, the human experience is a burden.

Dostoevsky, born in 1821, is considered a prophet of the Russian people. Famous for writing *Crime and Punishment* and *Anna Karenia*,

Dostoevsky, according to researcher Frank in his book *Dostoevsky: The Mantle of the Prophet,* [34] was a genius at portraying 'lower-class' man's struggle for freedom in which he managed to blend ideology and psychology. He had a profound ability to depict the deep wounds of human suffering.

Dostoevsky was compelled to write. That was his purpose. In doing so, he suffered immensely. Like Van Gogh, he had episodes in which he would lose his memory and, on occasion, injure himself. At times he was so low that he wrote, "I'm so miserable that – would you believe it? – I'm irritated that I haven't had an attack. If I'd at least hurt myself somehow in an attack, that would at least be some sort of diversion." [35] Dostoevsky was diagnosed with epilepsy. In his fits, he had profound visions, but with them came profound agitation. He wrote, "I haven't been able to sleep, I worry, sort through the chance [of an accident] pace around the room, have visions of the children, worry about [my wife], my heart pounds (I've had palpitations of the heart up these last three days)… It finally begins to dawn, and I sob, pace around the room and cry, with a sort of shaking (I don't understand it myself, it's never happened before.)" [36]

Dostoevsky, a great visionary, a man compelled to fulfill his destiny, suffered greatly. The burden of his human existence was at times too much to bear. We can look at the tremendous works of art created by both Van Gogh and Dostoevsky and marvel at their genius. We can be in awe of the tenacity of Joan of Arc. But deep down, they suffered. Their human experience, the human journey, was not an easy one.

In my own quest to fulfill my purpose, I struggle. Sometimes I look around at people who are enjoying a glass of wine, or walking hand in hand with a partner window shopping, or laughing uproariously at a joke and think, "I wish I could relax like those people and just settle into the human experience and enjoy it a bit more". But my purpose is my passion and it is my joy. I have many sleepless nights. When I am wrestling with a section in this book, a figure stands at the end of my bed and talks to me about what I am to write. Hours and hours go by as the messages are delivered. In the morning, I am exhausted.

Stressed-Out Soul Dominant

- Dominated by the need to serve God
- Feelings of inadequacy in efforts to live up to God's purpose
- Fear that God will be disappointed in efforts
- Single-minded, obsessive, and perfectionist attitudes about a project or idea become overwhelming
- Sleepless nights because of visions or worry
- Eating, exercise, personal appearance and hygiene may deteriorate
- Body deteriorates with illness
- May take on characteristics of schizophrenia, epilepsy, clinical depression, or obsessive/compulsive disorder
- May have thoughts of suicide

Parenting Implications

Soul Dominant characteristics may not be all that obvious in a child. I can really only speak about my own experience here and how I wanted to be parented. From the age of four, I wanted to be a teacher - I was instructed by the universe to do so. This is a very respectable profession, so my parents did not have much to worry about. However, my commitment to being a teacher was complicated by my ability to see spirits and have visions. I am finding out now, at forty-six years of age, that my commitment to being a teacher of the Spirit and Soul Aspect of the human being, is causing some concern for my family.

When I set out on my own after my divorce, I had the time to explore my understanding of spiritual matters. I went to Native sweat lodges, engaged in fasts and participated in four Sundance Ceremonies. I know that my family was worried that I was losing my mind and that I was going to enter into some sort of 'dark', cult-like spiritual group. My obsession to learn as much about my Spirit Aspect as I could, led to my pulling away from my family enough to create my own space to explore. They did not have spiritual experiences as I did. They were not kept awake at night with spirit visits. They could not send their spirit on errands for them. And they had never had two near death experiences. I was unique. I had to know the full extent of my spirit's capabilities.

Now I am trying to write my findings into this book. I toil for hours, giving up much of my spare time to fulfill my purpose. I do not think my family fully grasps the importance of this work to me. They ask me questions from time to time about how it is going. On occasion, I see their eyes glaze over when I launch into my excitement about my project. My older sister is always very encouraging, even though she makes it perfectly clear that she does not understand my experiences, but she fully respects my passion and desire to fulfill my purpose. That is good enough for me.

How can family and friends be supportive of a Soul Dominant child or sibling? I speak for myself, as a Soul Dominant individual when I say, "Simply respect my passion, invite me over for dinner to get me away from my computer, ask questions about my work, but let me have a break from my purpose by letting me do something frivolous like watch a funny film, or go out dancing. Understand that if my garden looks as if no one has tended it all summer that my garden is not my priority. Finishing my book is my priority. Do not be insulted if I can not join everyone for lunch out, but keep inviting me because sometimes I need time off."

Dostoevsky was fully supported by his wife. She understood his nature and would attempt to soothe him by listening to his visions and by alleviating his concerns by being a rock solid individual. Van Gogh did not have anyone who would comfort him about his earnest desire to please God, to be of service. The religious community in which he grew up did not support his desire to befriend the poor and give help when needed. Van Gogh's brother was the one solid in his life. They wrote letters most of their lives, giving each other encouragement. Van Gogh's obsessive desire to please God was relentless – but he eventually committed suicide. As for Joan of Arc, she grew up in a time when visions were considered normal. She did not view her ability and purpose odd or strange. However, her death came as a result of a power struggle as the

French people followed her more than the King. Jealousy led to her death - now she is a Saint.

For me, the key is to have respect for my passion. As long as I continue working at my respectable job as a high school teacher, raise my three children in a caring and effective manner and look after my house, I feel that in my spare time I can pursue this avenue of my purpose.

I have, however, set some boundaries. I will not let it get in the way of spending time with my children. I go to every sports match, school event and party related to my children's activities. We have lots of dinner parties with friends and family. We snuggle on the couch to watch movies and our favorite television shows; I bake their favorite snacks; we eat a home cooked dinner every night together and share our stories of the day; I jog or attend a fitness program most days. I write when they go to visit their Dad for the week-end, or in the early hours before they wake up. That is how I have established my own boundaries so that I do not slip into the Stressed-Out Soul Dominant category.

Characteristics of a Balanced Body, Mind, Spirit, and Soul

- exercises regularly, eats healthy meals, practices good hygiene
- keeps a relatively tidy home and work environment
- reads a lot, becomes educated and has some intellectual pursuits
- recognizes the spirit's desires and has learned how to discern between helpful desires and harmful ones
- has learned how to access spirit dimension for visions and how to turn it down when a break is needed
- has a strong sense of purpose to serve humankind
- has learned how to balance out, on a daily basis, needs of the body, the mind, the spirit and the soul

Overall Implications

The Soul Dominant individual is compelled to fulfill a divine purpose.

He or she feels guided by a force outside of the Self, a force that beckons them to serve humanity in a grand way. Others may dismiss the Soul Dominant person's passion as delusions of grandeur. They may think, "How could that person think that they can perform some great cause?" How could Joan of Arc, a tiny teen-ager think that she could save a country? How could a disheveled madman like Van Gogh think that he had any purpose whatsoever? He could not even pass school requirements, his painting skills were self-taught and he only sold one painting in his lifetime.

Soul Dominant people can have a very difficult human experience if they do not learn to balance out their Body, Mind and Spirit Aspects. They can suffer a great deal because they can become so overwhelmed with their purpose and their attempts to please God. They may never feel that they are doing enough. Being alone allows them to have visions. However, being alone can also contribute to their feelings of inadequacy as they wrestle with the visions that they perceive.

Body/Mind people may not understand the intensity of the Soul Dominant person and may label them as mentally ill. They can not understand the obsessive tendencies and the single-mindedness of the Soul Dominant. Quite often, the project that the Soul Dominant suffered for and toiled with is not given its just praise by the Body/Mind community until after death. Typically, the Soul Dominant person is working on a project that a Body/Mind person cannot even conceive of because that project came through a vision. The relevance of the project may take more years to come to fruition than the Soul Dominant person has years on Earth. Being misunderstood by society adds to the suffering of the Soul Dominant individual.

There is still one more aspect to consider and that is the God Aspect. This aspect allows us all to be connected by the Force of Oneness. Perhaps if we all tapped into this aspect within ourselves we could become more sensitive toward the Soul Dominant people of our society and less judgmental.

CHAPTER TWELVE

Developing Our God Aspect

It's really a wonder
That I haven't dropped all my ideals,
Because they seem so absurd
And impossible to carry out.
Yet I keep them,
Because in spite of everything,
I still believe
That people are really good at heart.[37]

Anne Frank (1929 – 1945) in *The Diary of A Young Girl*

∽

Despite Anne Frank's frightful existence and eventual death during the holocaust of World War II, evident in her *Diary of a Young Girl*, is the fact that she still managed to keep her God Aspect alive and well. She hung onto her ideal that human beings are essentially good and that we are all connected to each other through a divine connection.

When I was fully entranced by my vision four years ago, I did not receive information on God Dominance; therefore, I have titled this chapter, *Developing Our God Aspect*. In the years that have passed I have had plenty of opportunity to explore the concept of the God Aspect.

The God Aspect is one that recognizes that we are all connected through the Force of Oneness. A God Dominant person would be someone who was born with a strong desire to connect all human beings. I have not met anyone like this personally, but I have seen people develop their God Aspect as they go through their life's journey. The person that comes to mind as someone who has developed all five aspects would be Oprah Winfrey. I do not have time to watch her show every day, but the days that

I do watch, I am always struck by her ability to empathize with her guests. It is this ability that has made her as popular as she is.

Oprah knows that she has a purpose. She clearly attempts to fulfill her Spirit Aspect, her desires. She is an astute businesswoman; therefore, it is obvious that she has worked very hard to expand her Mind Aspect. Her Body Aspect is probably her weakest of the five. She admits that she struggles with weight, but really she looks fantastic. I am not certain Oprah was born God Dominant, or whether over the years she has come closer and closer to the Divine Force of Oneness. What I can make an observation on is that she is very conscious of her human evolution.

Catriona Lemay Doan, Canadian speed skating champion, is also very in touch with her God Aspect. Before every race, her husband would go way up to the top of the spectator risers to pray for not only her, but for all of the competitors. Her husband said that he prayed for everyone to have their best race ever and for all of the racers to complete the event safely. Both Lemay Doan and her husband were aware of the connection between themselves and the other racers. They were all one through their love of the sport and through the love of their families and friends. Is it possible that her highly developed God Aspect added that little bit extra to her tremendous hard work in training; that little bit extra to make her the world champion?

Lance Armstrong, the famous Tour de France champion has expanded his five aspects, I believe, rather unconsciously. On a talk show, he spoke openly about his growing up years. He was obviously very strong in his Body Aspect, in that he loved his bicycle from an early age. Of all the sports, his spirit desired cycling and that is what he pursued. Cycling is a rather solitary activity, an activity in which the individual must learn to overcome physical and mental pain in order to succeed. In my model, Lance Armstrong was high in both Body and Spirit Aspects because he would have had to tap into his Spirit Aspect in order to overcome the physical pain of driving his muscles to exhaustion.

When Armstrong was diagnosed with testicular cancer, his Soul Aspect came shining through to anchor him with his real purpose for being sent to Earth at this time in history. He was not only sent to Earth to win the Tour de France. He was sent here to inspire others to beat the odds of cancer through his 'Live Strong' campaign. He has offered hope and power to other sufferers of cancer. If you can see Armstrong's human evolution, you will see a Body Dominant person, with a strong Spirit Aspect, one that knew what it desired – cycling. That spirit enabled Armstrong to use his desire to promote his Soul purpose, 'Live Strong'. By doing so, Lance Armstrong survived.

I saw Armstrong being interviewed by Oprah after he won his final Tour de France. He gave us all a look at his home in France. He stopped at one room, which had become very meaningful to him. He said that he had found a church altar for sale and, for some odd reason, he had set it up in a small room in his home as a mini sanctuary. I knew right away that Lance Armstrong was ready to start expanding his God Aspect. He had a longing for a deeper connection to life and to his children. I do not think that Armstrong is aware, or fully conscious, of why he is doing what he is doing, but he fits nicely into my model of developing the five aspects of the human being. I hope some day I can find out what he learns about his God Aspect. I am only halfway through developing my Soul Aspect. Hopefully, I will be able to grow into my God Aspect, too.

I have not opened myself up completely to my God Aspect. But now that I know it is there, I feel excited to start the process. Four months ago, I started a new exercise program called Ripped™. It is a program, created by Jari Love, a fellow Calgarian, which combines weight training and cardio work. I have to say that it stimulated muscles that I did not know that I even had. When I go for my daily jog, I feel those new muscles at work. Now I am beginning to realize that there are Mind, Spirit, Soul, and God muscles that also need to be worked on, ones I do not know I have. I have been teaching people exercises that will assist them in developing the 'muscles' of their Spirit Aspect. I am excited about discovering the exercises that will stimulate the Soul and God muscles, as well.

Balancing the Body, Mind, Spirit, Soul and God Aspects

As we consider all five aspects of the human being, it is important to remember that no dominance is superior to another. In fact, you can draw yourself a pie graph and divide it into five equal parts. Label each part either Body (Physical), Mind (Intellectual), Spirit (Desires), Soul (Purpose), and God (Force of Oneness). Identify your starting point in life. Did you start out Body Dominant, Mind Dominant, Spirit Dominant or Soul Dominant? What is your next dominant aspect? I am Soul Dominant, then Spirit, Mind, Body and God. Therefore, on my pie graph, I will put my pencil on Soul Dominance, then draw my arrow going to the next piece – Spirit Dominance, then to Mind, around to Body, then God.

Color in each piece of pie the amount that you feel you have accomplished to date. Are you 20%, 60%, 80% happy with how you have developed your Body Aspect? What about your Mind Aspect? Are you satisfied, or should you read more books, or take some courses? Once you have colored in your pie, insert activities that you do to prove that you are developing any one of your particular aspects. At the bottom of your page, list some goals and strategies that you intend to fulfill to strengthen each one of your aspects. Remember that you have all five aspects and your personal development requires that you expand them all. The idea is to have fun with the human experience; to enjoy the exquisiteness of being human.

CHAPTER THIRTEEN

The Quest for Understanding Spirit

A man might contemplate God, might live God, and be united, through meditation and ecstasy, with the essence of the universe, provided he escaped from the shackles of the body. It is not a question of the intellectual knowledge of God, but of illumination.[38]

Alain Hus's interpretation of *Neo Platonism in Greek and Roman Religion*

༄

In explaining this new theory of Body, Mind, Spirit and Soul Dominance, it is important to place it in the context of what already exists in the realm of spiritual understanding; to bring a greater sense of perspective to my vision. For thousands of years, people have been on a quest to understand the human spirit. I have found that to some Mind/Body Dominant people, my theory seems a little far-fetched, but as Alain Hus demonstrates in his interpretation of *Neo Platonism in Greek and Roman Religion,* the study of spirit cannot be just an intellectual activity.

Last year, while at my school jurisdiction's annual Teacher's Convention, I was locked out of a session on student giftedness. It was filled to capacity when I got there. I wanted to attend to find out if, in the year 2005, researchers in education were at last including spiritual giftedness, for the Spirit Dominant individuals, as a learning style. I was marginally upset about being excluded from this discussion of giftedness, as I was really keen to raise the issue of the Spirit Dominant learner.

Another teacher stood disappointed outside the door with me. It was too late at that time to get to another session, so I asked him if he wanted to join me for a coffee and discuss why we were both attracted to that particular session. So there I was, explaining my Dominance Theory to a physics teacher of gifted and talented high school students who had never heard of spiritual giftedness, let alone Spirit Dominance. Furthermore, he was a scientist and could not accept the 'fact' that there could be an alternate reality of a spiritual dimension. To his mind, human beings did not have a Spirit Aspect. That is when I launched into the scientific, neurological and genetic research, which supports the idea of Spirit Dominance. By the time the conversation was over, he had not only shared several of his own personal spiritual experiences that he had previously discounted as creative imagination, but we also set up a plan to do a research study together regarding the Spirit Aspect in the classroom.

The human spirit has long been a fascinating topic of study and there are countless sources to draw from. The scientific evidence for Spirit Dominance is overwhelming, but as a point of reference, I would like to start with the insights and wisdom of the first documented 'great thinkers' – the philosophers.

The Greek Philosophers

There have been many great philosophers and incredibly gifted thinkers that have offered their views and insights into the human condition over the course of time. For many of the early philosophers, their ideas went out of fashion and were disregarded because their understandings could not be validated with scientific evidence. With the modern technological age, scientists are on the edge of empirically proving the existence of the human spirit. That is why I want to swing back to a historical time when philosophical thought was in abundance.

I have only begun to understand what Plato and Socrates envisioned about the human soul, now that I am an adult. When I took my first philosophy course way back in my undergraduate degree studies, I had no idea that we were talking about the human spirit, even though at that point I had just had my first near-death experience. Philosophy, in those days, was taught according to logic – the 'if this is true, then that is true', kind of logic. We were never asked if we had spiritual experiences of our own, if we had a personal understanding of our own spirit.

Hearnshaw gives a fairly comprehensive overview of the 'great big thinkers' in the book *The Shaping of Modern Psychology.*[39] In it, I learned that Plato (428-348 B.C.) visualized the soul as dynamic, each level possessing its own drives and its own desires. I have found this to be true. We can continue to expand our spirits and souls, just as we can expand our body's muscles and flexibility through exercise and our mind through study and discipline. Plato's teacher, Socrates, believed that the care of the soul was man's most important task.[40] I would have to agree, except that I find that the caring for the body and mind are of equal importance for the Spirit Dominant individual. Also, my vision told me that the spirit and the soul are not the same thing. The soul is a higher aspect than our spirit.

Aristotle (384-322 B.C.) viewed the soul and body as not two substances, but two aspects of reality.[41] His vision and mine are very similar. Indeed, we have aspects to us. They are not separate entities. According to my vision, we can interact with our environment through our five different aspects, body, mind, spirit, soul and God. As human beings, however, we are not always certain which aspect we are using in response to our environment.

Plotinus (204-270 A.D.) viewed the body as simply an instrument for the soul and according to him, the soul is indeed separate from the body.[42] The familiar saying, "We are spirits having a human experience", can be attributed to Plotinus. My vision expanded Plotinus' ideas for it revealed that not all spirits enjoy having a human experience and not all humans recognize that they have a spirit and a soul.

Diogenes (412 B.C.), one of my favorite Greek philosophers, argued that our mission on Earth is to come to terms with our own being. "All knowledge is self-knowledge", he believed and, "Self-mastery is the only liberty worthwhile."[43] I completely agree with Diogenes here in that we must come to terms with all five aspects of our human experience.

We must learn how to fulfill our potential in every aspect and when we feel a weakness, we can set goals to try to overcome it. We would be wise to recognize when it is necessary to activate a different aspect to maintain balance and achieve mastery in all aspects.

Epicurus is another philosopher I admire, as well. He founded the hedonist school, in which the pleasure of being alive was revered. "Today we are alive," he said, "and this is all the certainty we have. So let us make the best of our present existence."[44] Epicurians were materialistic. They did not believe in a divine order of the universe and basically believed that humans should grasp as much happiness as they can. He must have been the motivation behind the idea that we are not here for a long time, we are here for a good time.

My Body Dominant sister, Sandra, is a huge inspiration to me. She really knows how to enjoy the sensual experiences of being a human being. Her meals are so visually pleasing and they are prepared with the most flavorful ingredients. She knows how to set the atmosphere in her home for maximum enjoyment. Sandra and I cannot be more different, but I so enjoy her enthusiasm for life. I have never met anyone who enjoys a vacation more than my sister. I totally agree with Epicurus in his Body Dominant observation - we are meant to enjoy the human experience. It is not all about work, or the search for meaning. It is also about Fun!

My older sister and I used to spend a week together every summer after I got divorced. I would fly to Montreal, where she lives and together we would go off on a girl's vacation, usually to Stowe, Vermont. Sandra's friend would lend us her cabin in Stowe, which was a wonderful retreat for us. I remember arriving, loaded down with bags of groceries, lots of wine and our hiking gear. Sandra is Body Dominant and has now become my mentor for enjoying the human experience. Instantly, she had all of the groceries put away, tea made and had miraculously pulled out a box of chocolate almond bark to signify that we were 'officially' on vacation, no rules, no diets, no phone calls, no boundaries.

My epiphany came when Sandra stretched out on the living room couch and carefully wrapped the blanket that had been hung over the arm of the sofa around her, tucking it in so that she was completely comfortable. I sat perched on the very edge of the armchair, barely making physical contact with it. I looked at my sister, so absolutely at home under someone else's blanket, on someone else's couch and under someone else's roof. I thought, "The difference between my sister and I is that she is at home everywhere and I am at home nowhere." Because Sandra is Body Dominant, she relishes in the creature comforts of being alive, whereas I, at that point in my life, never relaxed enough in my physical surroundings to enjoy them. Since this epiphany, with my sister's annual week in the summer mentorship, I think that I have made huge gains in relishing the exquisiteness of being a human being.

I do, however, continue to have difficulty with people who do not accept the spiritual nature of the human being. Sometimes I regard what a Body Dominant person values, like a perfectly groomed lawn, as trivial compared to what I am working on. I admit it! I must learn to value the physical, tangible parts of existence even more and take pleasure in these tasks of beauty. And I can, as long as my quest for activating my spirit and soul dimensions is valued. Friendships, for me, do not last long if my understandings of spirit are considered trivial. Therefore, as my personal development continues, I am learning to indulge more in the Body Aspect of myself. (I even bought new work-out clothes for my 'Ripped' class!)

The Age of Reason

The Age of Reason brought out the Mind Aspect of most people. At this time, all truth had to be proven empirically - experienced through the five senses. Francis Bacon (1561-1626) argued that man should get out of the cavern of self to understand universal truths, not just individual ones. The true scientist, the true philosopher, must recognize the limitations of his own viewpoint. In the true Mind Dominant perspective, Bacon is famous for stating, "My heart must believe only what my mind can prove."

Baruch Spinoza (1632-1677), however, argued that the soul is imprisoned by the physical body. In his Spirit Dominant view, he believed that the human being is limited by its five senses and that we only catch glimpses of the divine whole. He concluded that we only have a puny intelligence compared to the infinite intelligence of God and that our destiny is greater than we think. He argued that we are all in different grades, depending upon our mental and spiritual development.

Spinoza echoes what I have heard from several Spirit Dominant individuals. They feel imprisoned by the body. That is why they need to retreat to a quiet place to let the spirit soar. I agree with his view that we are all in different grades. However, according to my theory, spiritual development is not the be all and end all. A person may have a high grade in spirit, if he is actually using his spirit to acquire knowledge, rather than just lying around in bed all day, sleeping life away. He may need to improve his grade in Body Aspect development and start to eat and enjoy nutritious foods, take care of personal appearance and exercise regularly. Personal development is about expanding all aspects of ourselves and not viewing the body as a prison, or even just a tool, but as a medium to delight in and savor the human experience.

The ancient philosophers and the Renaissance thinkers offered wonderful ideas that were useful to people in their daily lives. Discussion of man's spiritual nature fell out of favor during the Age of Reason because no one could empirically prove the existence of God, or the existence of a spiritual dimension. Belief in these ideas began to fall under the category of superstition. Recently, however, advanced technology has begun to prove that man is indeed 'hard-wired' for spirit. Our brain composition and our genetic make-up may very well be the explanation for why some people are Spirit Dominant and others are not.

Spirit and the Theory of Evolution

The late Dr. Hardy and his successor Dr. Hay, both zoologists and Darwinians, came to the conclusion after decades of research that those who consciously developed their spiritual side had a better chance of survival than people who did not. Both scientists argued that for man to evolve and survive, he must recognize how his own spirit could allow him to escape danger, discover the riches he needs to stay alive and, ultimately, remain hopeful in light of obstacles that may present themselves.

My main concern is that we are doing a disservice to our children by not consciously nurturing their Spirit and Soul Aspect. By wiring them up with cell phones and high speed internet, are we destroying their ability to use their intuition as a problem solving mechanism? I believe that teachers and parents must become more aware of the Spirit Aspect of students. This part of them is a survival tool and should be nurtured.

CHAPTER FOURTEEN

Scientific Evidence for Spirit and Soul

John laughs at me, of course, but one expects that in marriage.
John is practical in the extreme. He has no patience with faith, an intense
horror of superstition, and he scoffs openly at any talk of things not to be
felt and seen and put down in figures.[45]

Charlotte Perkins Gilman (1860 – 1935) in her short story
The Yellow Wallpaper

༉

The main character of *The Yellow Wallpaper* is a writer and when her husband moves her into a rented home, she has an odd feeling about it. She sees ghostly figures of women, but her husband denies her visions and instead puts her on medication to control her 'nerves'.

Neurological Explanation

Persinger (1987), a neurologist in Canada, designed a controversial mechanism to evoke spiritual experiences in his subjects.[46] He created a helmet that would direct electromagnetic impulses into the brain. He soon discovered that when impulses were directed at the right temporal lobe of any individual, that individual would indeed envision a loved one who had passed away, hear voices, have a conversation with God, or engage in some other spiritual experience including communing with aliens. Persinger tried the helmet on himself and he, too, had a spiritual experience. Yet, before this experiment he had never had such a vision. Persinger's goal was not to demean anyone's religious or mystical experiences, but to examine which portions of the brain generate the experience.

Two schools of thought emerged from Persinger's research. One is that mystical experiences, such as the ones that I have had, are nothing more than a misfiring in the right temporal lobe of the brain. I am not sure why my brain would be misfiring when I heard the voice that I was to become a teacher. Or why, when I was about ten years old, I heard a voice say, "Thirty-six. Die of breast cancer. You will miss your Mom." Or how my mother was certain that she felt me beside her while I cleaned out the cancer, even though I was thousands of miles away, sitting in a chair, visualizing her organs, tissue, bones, blood, and skin. This could not possibly be the result of a misfiring of the brain.

The second school of thought is that the human brain is hard-wired with a 'God Spot' and the right temporal lobe is the part of the brain specifically designed to engage in spiritual thought. I suppose that some people may have a more highly developed right temporal lobe and, therefore, are able to conceive of tremendous spiritual insights. I go a step further, however, and argue that some people's Spirit Aspect, not their brain, is more highly developed or highly active. I believe that some people's Spirit Aspect, that intangible part of them that will leave their physical body at the point of death and go to another dimension, is very strong and this strength gives these people who are Spirit Dominant capacities that Body/Mind Dominant people must learn to exercise. Spirit Dominant people do not need to put on Persinger's helmet to have an experience with spirit. But, the helmet itself proves that every human's brain has the potential to experience spirit. Since various parts of the brain control body movement and intellectual abilities, Persinger's research suggests that there is a link between the Spirit Aspect and a highly attuned right temporal lobe.

Many scientists regard the near-death experience as a malfunction of the brain. They believe that the similar stories told by those who have nearly died is simply a response to the brain shutting down. Melvin Morse, a pediatrician and author of the book *Where God Lives*,[47] is also one of the key researchers of near-death experiences. He has found that most of the participants in his study encounter a blast of pure, unconditional love when their consciousness merged with the light waiting for them at the point of death. Qualitative research evidence points to a universe that is a loving one, designed to nurture consciousness. Why do we take this reassuring version of truth away from people? My near-death experience followed exactly the format that Morse details in his book. I know that my experience was more than just a misfiring in my brain. However, I can imagine for those who have never experienced this euphoric sensation, that they may find it beyond their intellectual comprehension.

Another interesting observation that Morse makes about the participants in his study, namely children, is that once these children had their near-death experience, they took on new characteristics. They became more compassionate, more interested in understanding their mystical experience by reading heavily on the topic. They became more focused in school and, surprisingly, ate more healthy food. I found this interesting because in my theory, people are born Spirit Dominant, but according to Morse, people can open up their spiritual capacity as a result of a near-death. This makes sense to me.

We have all five aspects and our job in the human experience is to develop all five to their full potential. Imagine, once again, your pie graph divided into five sections: body, mind, spirit, soul and God. Our job is to fulfill our potential in each, regardless of our starting point, Body, Mind, Spirit, Soul, or God.

Ramachandran and Blakeslee (1998) venture into the arena of spirituality in their book *Phantoms of the Brain*, [48] but rather than accepting the notion that humans can have naturally occurring spiritual experiences, they focus on the phenomenon of epileptic seizures. Of particular interest to them is what happens to the brain when a piece of it becomes damaged through a disease or an accident. An epileptic seizure, which typically occurs in the temporal lobes, can trigger, for some patients, the perception of a spiritual experience such as a communion with God, or a profound sense of truth or insight. Neither one of these researchers was surprised at Persinger's discovery with respect to the electromagnetic stimulation of the temporal lobe. They found that some people have a 'temporal lobe personality', in which they have heightened emotions and see "cosmic significance in trivial events." According to them, these people tend to be humorless, full of self-importance and keep elaborate diaries that record experiences.

I admit I was rather insulted, at first, at the description of the 'temporal lobe personality'. I keep elaborate journals of my ideas and encourage others to do the same. I keep track of my insights before they slip away. Gelb (2002) found that a common trait of geniuses is that they see a relationship between seemingly unrelated events and also keep diaries of the ideas that randomly pop into their heads.[49] Personally, I do not believe in coincidence. I see every single encounter as having cosmic significance. I am fully committed to introducing people to their Spirit, Soul and God Aspects. In fact, I hope that someday I can have Spirit and Soul Dominance designated as a learning style in our education systems. Although I exhibit many of the characteristics of temporal lobe personality, I believe that it is these characteristics that have allowed me to come up with a fresh, new way to view human development.

I am also of the opinion that 'temporal lobe personality' is actually Spirit or Soul Dominance. I believe that people who have a very active right temporal lobe do perceive the universe differently than Body and Mind Dominant people, not better, just different. I think that people whose right temporal lobe is more developed, can reach out of the prison of the body and the five senses, and perceive some of the universal truths of our time. But, I also believe that some people's Spirit Aspect is more highly developed. St. Paul, Muhammad, Joan of Arc and Dostoyevsky all exhibited signs of epilepsy and they are some of our greatest visionaries.

Newberg and D'Aquila (1999), who study the neuro-psychology of religious experience, discovered that Buddhist meditators activated brain areas associated with intense concentration while the posterior superior parietal lobe, which determines the boundary of the body, became completely dead.[50] The meditators felt as though they had transcended their physical form during their concentrated meditation. This discovery suggests that humans have the capacity to activate and deactivate parts of the brain and, in this case, experience the spiritual at will. Therefore, Newberg and D'Aquila address the idea of which experience is 'more real', the state of meditation, or the 'normal' state. They decided that it does not really matter. If a person experiences a heightened state of consciousness through meditation, the experience is very real for the person. Their findings confirm my idea that the human being can open up other aspects to themselves, other than just the body and mind. Human beings can open up to the Spirit, Soul and God Aspects if they learn how.

Genetic Research

Hamer (2004), a geneticist, made a remarkable discovery that some people have DNA that allows them to experience the spiritual, while others do not.[51] At first, he embarked on an elaborate sibling study to find out about addiction to cigarette smoking. He had siblings fill in a pen and pencil questionnaire. Imbedded in the questionnaire were distraction questions, primarily from Cloninger's self-transcendence test. Cloninger is a physician-scientist and professor of psychiatry, genetics and psychology at Washington University School of Medicine in St. Louis. He convinced Hamer that spirituality is a measurable quantity. His self-transcendence test is a product of his strong belief that spirituality can be measured.

Cloninger identified three character traits of individuals who were able to transcend their physical being. The first one is self-forgetfulness. People who have this component appear to lose track of time when they go into 'the zone'. They experience flashes of insight or understandings and are creative, original thinkers, as they see ordinary things as fresh and new. However, to the observer this person appears absent-minded.

The second component is transpersonal identification. The person feels a connectedness to the universe with a heightened sensual appreciation of what is seen, heard, smelled, touched and tasted. Thirdly, a spiritually-oriented person has a fascination with mysticism, things that cannot be explained by science. Incidentally, women scored 18% higher than men on the self-transcendent scale.

Once Hamer administered the addictions survey, with the self-transcendence scale imbedded, to thousands of participants, it suddenly dawned on him to isolate the results of the self-transcendence scale and compare the results of siblings. He made a remarkable discovery. He isolated the VMAT2 gene as the 'God Gene'. The VMAT2 gene can have an A attached to it, or a C. People born with VMAT2AA appear to have no interest whatsoever with spiritual ideas, as outlined on the self-transcendence test. People born with VMAT2CC tend to verge on an obsession with spiritual ideas. I guess that might explain a little more about me. Those born with VMAT2AC have a moderate interest in the spiritual.

Hamer's discovery suggests that some people are born genetically predisposed to a desire or lack of desire for understanding the spiritual, philosophical matters of life. In Hamer's study, 28% of the participants had the VMAT2 gene variant containing a C, compared to 72% carrying an A. But because both the C/C and C/A genotypes had increased self-transcendence scores, compared to the A/A genotype, it worked out that 47% of the people in his study were in the higher spirituality group.

Hamer's study is intriguing in another way. Since his was a sibling study, he set out the example of one male in his study, who had a VMAT2AA gene and had no interest in spiritual matters, preferring the world of business and finance. Meanwhile his brother carried the VMAT2CC gene and was compelled to become a Buddhist monk. I use Hamer's discovery to prove that some people are born Spirit Dominant (VMAT2CC), while others are Body or Mind Dominant, with either some interest in spirit (VMAT2AC) or no interest (VMAT2AA). Hamer's ideas on spirit can be found in his book called, *The God Gene: How Faith is Hardwired into Our Genes.*

The only contradiction I see with Hamer's theory is that other research studies, like Morse's, have shown that if a person has a mystical experience, such as a near-death experience, they very often become a changed individual. They often take up an obsession with understanding the nature of their spiritual experience. Possibly these people are VMAT2AC. There are some people who have had near-death experiences, but do not recall any mystical experience. Maybe they are incapable and are VMAT2AA.

According to my Body, Mind, Spirit, Soul Dominance theory, however, everyone has a Spirit Aspect - it is just that not everyone is conscious of the fact. I understand that whether a person believes it or not, they have a spirit. At the point of death, the spirit will leave the body and go to a place of unconditional love.

A Mind Dominant Perspective

Alper (2000) attempted to prove, using the brain research just mentioned, that while humans believe they have spiritual experiences, they are, in fact, only experiencing electrical misfirings in the brain. He began his book, *The "God" Part of the Brain*,[52] by revealing his own quest to achieve a spiritual experience. He traveled, meditated and even took drugs. The end result was severe clinical depression, which was alleviated by more drugs. Therefore, he came to the conclusion that since he could not personally achieve spiritual experiences, as others claimed to have, that these happenings must simply be chemically induced somehow in the brain. Perhaps Alper was born with the VMAT2AC gene, which would allow him to be interested in spirituality, but not have a profound personal experience. It is rather arrogant for Alper to dismiss the experiences others have had. Hardy, in his extensive research project, found that spiritual experiences had a profound impact on his participants and have been known to have survival value.

Conclusion

The technological age has now been able to discover that the brain is indeed hard-wired for spiritual experiences and, that when stimulated, everyone can have a profound encounter with the mystical. This confirms to me that we do indeed have a Spirit Aspect and that if we learn how to naturally stimulate the right temporal lobe, we too can gain insight into the universal truths. When I came home from my *Philosophy of Mind* class that Friday afternoon, turned out the lights, unplugged the telephone, lit a candle, nestled myself on my living room couch, settled my mind of distraction and posed the question, "How are the body, mind and spirit connected?", I believe that I activated my Spirit Aspect, rather than my right temporal lobe in order to receive the Body, Mind, Spirit, Soul Dominance Theory. However, I am open to the possibility that the Spirit Aspect and the brain are inter-related.

Hamer's genetic study proves to me that some people are born Spirit Dominant. This explains why my brother and sister have very little to no interest in spiritual matters while I am obsessed with the spiritual domain. More importantly, the brain-based and genetic research demonstrates that there is a spiritual side to the human being.

As a classroom teacher, I see this side in my students. They want to talk about their experiences. Many of them want to develop their Spirit Aspect as rigorously as they develop their Body and Mind Aspects. But, in our current education system, the study of the Spirit Aspect is relatively non-existent. I am sure there are teachers like myself who try to nurture the spiritual understandings of students, without using a religious model. But we keep these discussions low key, in the closet, so to speak.

When I get a knock on my classroom door during lunch hour and a student wants to share a spiritual experience that is haunting, I cannot help but put down whatever I am working on and assist this student in understanding his or her spiritual insights. When the happy, sparkly look in a student's eyes disappears, I have to ask them what happened. The spirit is stuck someplace and this student needs to know how to bring it back inside the body. When a student is suffering through the human experience, hating the physical, tangible expectations of society and of having a body, I cannot sit back and watch him suffer. We talk. When a student appears late every day, exhausted from lack of sleep, we talk. Invariably, he or she is kept awake at night listening to voices and having visions. Turning on the radio helps tune out the voices, but they need spiritual tools to help manage the visions. Unfortunately, many of these students are given medication instead. They medicate their visions away instead of learning how to use the visions to better their own lives and the lives of members of our society.

In 2001, Bibby ran a national survey on Canada's teens.[53] He discovered that 78% of teens believed in life after death; 76% identified with near-death experiences; and 63% had personally envisioned an event before it happened. His study was much more in-depth than what is isolated here. The findings overwhelmingly suggest that teens are highly interested in spiritual matters and that our education systems must find a way to address student curiosities on the subject.

I believe it is about time that we have a call for action. People have spiritual experiences. We can no longer hide these experiences away in a closet. Some people are suffering as a result of their ability to connect with a spiritual dimension. Yet, teachers, parents, physicians and mental health workers are not getting the necessary training to deal with the spiritual trauma many people go through. We would rather pretend that this side of the human being does not exist. Brain research and genetic studies now show that humans do have a Spirit Aspect. We must start implementing a spiritual component into our teaching practices. We must start understanding the characteristics of a spiritual trauma. We must learn how to nurture the spiritual aspect of our children.

Recently, I submitted a proposal to speak at our city-wide teachers' convention. My topic was *Spiritual Intelligence: How to Nurture Spirit Through Our Teaching*. It was rejected. In the body of my proposal, I listed the neurological evidence for spirit and the need for teachers to become more familiar with adolescent spirituality. My mission is to gather support to urge school boards and medical practitioners to include the Spirit, Soul and God Aspects into their models of delivery. This aspect of the human being is atrophying in many people. As a result, they are feeling sad, isolated, purposeless and ineffective. I urge these people to build their spirit, soul and God muscles rather than reach for a bottle of medication. I urge parents and teachers to nurture the natural spiritual insights our children have. Dignify these experiences as part of their natural human evolution.

PART FOUR
Developmental Disorders

CHAPTER FIFTEEN
Spiritual Developmental Disorders

Infant Joy…Pretty joy!
Sweet joy but two days old,
Sweet joy I call thee:
Thou dost smile,
I sing the while,
Sweet joy befall thee! [54]

William Blake (1757 – 1827) in *Infant Joy*

ॐ

William Blake looks at a sweet newborn and is filled with joy for this innocent new being. While I was immersed in my vision, I asked the voice what the practical applications for this theory were in terms of human development. Again, I was very surprised by the response. I had never thought of the human spirit in such a way before.

What was revealed to me is that there can be EXTREMELY Spirit Dominant people. There are those who go far beyond the characteristics of the stressed-out Spirit Dominant types. Stressed-out Spirit Dominant people, for the most part, can still function in the physical world. The message I received was that just as there are some people who are very sure that they have a body and a mind, but no spirit, there are some people who live on Earth in spirit, but not in mind or body. These intensely Spirit Dominant people have difficulty functioning in the human dimension and are not filled with the joy that William Blake describes in his poem *Infant Joy*.

When any gorgeous, tiny infant is born, we assume that he or she actually desires to be welcomed in our loving embrace. We assume that this newly emerging human being is ready to leave the peaceful, euphoric realm of unconditional love into a noisy, harsh and, at times, abrasive life as a human. Imagine being ripped away from the realm of brilliant love, a dimension where there is no physical pain or disease to live here on Earth. The infant's first experience is a painful journey down the birth canal, a brisk entry into a realm with bright, artificial lights, where all is suddenly cold and where gasping for air becomes a means to survival. Rough cloth is wrapped around the body and the newborn is whisked away to a cold, metal tray to be weighed and measured. A doctor leans over with a bright light, examining his body for any malformations. When satisfied, a nurse handles him and plops him in his mother's arms and the mother is urged to start breastfeeding. If the mother has never breastfed before, the wee one has to work extra hard to coax the milk to release.

Now, a Body Dominant baby, who is ready to take on the human form and is excited to enjoy the physical, sensual parts of being human, would likely not have such a problem with the transition from spiritual dimension to this earthly plane. They came to Earth to enjoy the human experience. But for a Spirit Dominant baby, the entry into the human journey may very well be painful. Struggling to eat is painful; the rough touch of clothing and human hands, no matter how loving, is painful; noise, even if it is the voice of an adoring parent, is painful.

These Spirit Dominant babies may very well react in one of two ways. They may screech and holler when they are forced to struggle for food, or they may wrestle and cry when diapers are changed, when they are dressed, or bathed. To these babies, the body is not a source of pleasure. It is a source of pain. Later, these babies may reject any new food, pablum or solids. They are fussy about wearing the same shirt every day, eating the same food and following the same routine. Once they find something that is not painful, they do not want to give it up. This can be exasperating for a parent who has a child that screeches so much of the time, is always fussy, a child who is really struggling with taking on the human form.

The other reaction a newly born child may have is to retreat altogether from the human dimension. He may appear limp and unresponsive to noise, faces, or movement. Basically, he is saying, "You can give me a body, but I am not going to use it." This baby, as he grows older, may prefer to live in a world of his own, a spirit world, in which he allows his Spirit Aspect to continue interacting with the spiritual dimension, while his body remains rather inactive on Earth. He may appear to sleep, or stare off into space for enormous lengths of time. If forced to come back to Earth, to come back into his body, he may shriek and cry, preferring to remain uninterrupted in his spirit world.

What I learned from my vision is that not everyone has the desire to take on the human form. Just as there can be physical or mental birth defects, there can be spiritual birth defects. I do not particularly like the word 'defect', but it is the only one that I can think of that most aptly describes the essence of the message that I was given.

We assume that this little soul, who comes into the world after hours of painful contractions, is delighted to take on the human form. The vision revealed to me that some newborns would rather stay in the spiritual dimension, or heaven, or whatever the realm is called where our spirit resides before it is called into a human body; before it is called upon to be born on a certain date, to a certain family, with a certain story. Some babies' spirits would rather stay in the euphoric, unconditional love plane that I went to in my second near-death experience.

When I heard this message, my own son's story of how God told him that he had to come down to be a human, made even more sense. It got me thinking that perhaps there are some spirits who are not as obliging as my son. Alex said that he did not want to come down and be a human, especially to be a son of a 'mean' faced mother. I realize now that there must be some spirits who have come to Earth ill-prepared, or resistant to taking on the human body. They may have come to Earth kicking and screaming. Or they have come to Earth not realizing that they are even human.

We have all heard tell of spirits, or ghosts, who roam the Earth not knowing that their body is dead. If this is true, then it must be equally true that some spirits roam the Earth not knowing that they are alive in Body and Mind. As I mentioned, when my son was born, his delivery was very precarious. The obstetrician managed to manipulate him around so that he presented feet first, but by the time my son made it into the arms of the doctor, he was blue and not breathing. With the medical team working on him, Alex started breathing.

I often wonder, though, if we all engage in a "conversation with God" before our spirit enters our body. I wonder if my son resisted his birth into the human dimension. Perhaps he really did not want to be born. While I was absorbing this information during the vision, it suddenly dawned on me that babies who die of SIDS, sudden infant death syndrome, have decided to go back to the place they came, the one where life is so free and easy without a body. I mentioned earlier that, as a child, I used to lie on my bed and find breathing so difficult that I would force myself to keep breathing. I now believe that these little babies with SIDS simply stopped breathing and their spirits returned to the spiritual dimension.

My son's conversation with God implies that the spirit is that part of us that had the conversation with God before our arrival on earth. The spirit is the intangible part of us and the soul has a purpose and meaning. As the spirit enters at birth, it departs at death, presumably to reconnect with God in another plane. However, there are some children born who are not as agreeable as my son. There are some babies born who do not want to take on the human form.

Autism

My vision revealed to me that autistic children are the ones who are so far Spirit Dominant that they do not recognize or accept that they have a body. Just as some body /mind people recognize that they only have a body and a mind, not a spirit, autistic children either do not realize that they have a body, or cannot connect with their bodies. Some people cannot connect with their spirit and need to put on Persinger's helmet to have an experience. I now realize that some Spirit Dominant people cannot connect with their mind or body.

At the time of the vision, I did not know much about autism. I went to the university library and checked out some books on the subject, attended some educational presentations on autistic children and visited the autistic treatment center in my city. I found out that autistic children tend to live in a world of their own, not connecting with people. As infants, they can be very irritable, not eating, not sleeping and not allowing any clothes to be put on. They cry most of the time. Other autistic babies have been known to lie limp in their cribs, completely disengaged. As these children grow older, they continue to live in a world of their own, not making eye contact and not talking. They can take on repetitive behaviors like spinning, or clapping, or banging their heads. Many have difficulty handling any sort of change and can become angry if something in their environment is new or moved. Autism may not show up until a child is two years old. Sometimes a child may be able to experience a breakthrough and learn to cope with his or her environment and the people in it.

Of course, what I have described here is very general information about autism. Since no one can get inside the minds of these autistic children, the theories that abound are based on observation of behaviors and physical chemical tests, like blood samples. According to my vision, autistic children are either extremely angry at being given a body, or are basically saying, "You can give me a body, but I am not going to use it." The fact that autistic children find eating and sleeping painful fits with my theory and the fact that many autistic children find clothes itchy and uncomfortable also fits in with the idea that they have a hard time living within human skin.

I found out that the right temporal lobe can be stimulated by repetitive action. Spinning is the ritual adopted by the Whirling Dervishes of Russia. They spin as a way of reaching a spiritual state of euphoria. Many religious rituals rely on drumming as a means to excite a spiritual experience. Native Canadians, in particular, use drumming in a sweat lodge and in their Sundance Ceremony, as part of their spiritual practice. Drumming, tapping and banging the head excite the temporal lobe. Once we understand this, the behaviors of autistic children who engage in some sort of ritualistic repetitive action makes more sense. They engage in these behaviors because it allows them to stay in the spiritual dimension.

My cousin is a social worker. She operates a home for unmanageable children and adults. I telephoned her to pass my theory by her because she and I both have highly developed Spirit Aspects. She said that she had an autistic boy in her treatment center at the time and that he would only behave for her. One day she simply thought, "I think I'll take Robbie for an ice cream." When she looked over at him, he got up, went to the closet, got his coat out and stood beside her, ready to go. He had picked up her message telepathically.

I made an appointment to visit my city's autistic treatment center to talk to an expert on autism. She liked the theory, but thought it seemed too simple. I am wondering, though, what would happen if the experts had the children sit in a room with high Spirit Dominant people, the ones who can speak telepathically? Could the Spirit Dominant individuals communicate with these children and explain to them that they are human and that being human can be fun? I think it is worth a try.

So far, the experts have discarded the idea that autistic children come from 'cold' families. They see a link between autism and vaccinations. There is another link with food allergies. I read recently that university educated parents have more incidents of having an autistic child than non-university educated. What we do know for sure is that more and more autistic children are being diagnosed. Is this occurring because diagnostic procedures are in place and autism as a developmental disability is high profile these days? Or are more children opting out of the human experience, as my theory suggests? Are the physical and intellectual demands of humans becoming so great that children are rebelling, preferring to stay in the peaceful world that they have created?

Schizophrenia

The vision told me that schizophrenic people walk in two dimensions at the same time, earthly and spiritual. They need to be taught how to negotiate between the two. Again, the scientific, Mind Dominant community uses the five senses to understand the schizophrenic mind. People suffering from this 'mental illness' might have delusions of grandeur, believing that they can talk to God. They may hear voices, sometimes nasty ones that tell them to do evil things. They may see people or objects that are not 'really' there.

I believe that I have received this vision from an alternate reality. Despite not having a degree in medicine or psychiatry, I have discovered a theory that could radically change the school and medical systems. I hear voices, sometimes even nasty ones, but I just tell them to get lost. I have seen things that others cannot. Am I schizophrenic? No. However, if a person cannot distinguish between the spiritual realm and the human physical realm, then there is a problem. They must be helped and protected. But has any treatment plan ever included the idea that perhaps they are seeing things that are there, that only they have access to?

John Nash, the famous Nobel Prize mathematician and subject of the movie *A Beautiful Mind*, is a famous schizophrenic. A distinguished colleague asked him once how he could be a man of science and believe that he could hear the voices of aliens. He replied, "Because the ideas I had about supernatural beings came to me the same way that my mathematical ideas did. So I took them seriously."[55] He attributed his genius to his ability to connect with a spiritual realm. John Nash was most likely Spirit Dominant and needed to learn how to adjust to the human dimension.

Albert Einstein was never considered schizophrenic, but he was considered an eccentric. He received his theory of relativity through a vision. He stood on a cliff and imagined what it would be like to ride on a sunbeam. That was the birth of his theory of relativity. Furthermore, none of the geniuses mentioned above could fare very well in school, preferring to commit to self-directed study. I am not sure whether Joan of Arc went to school.

Even Bobby Fischer, genius American chess player, was considered an eccentric and in a recent newspaper article by Gabriel Schoenfeld, I read that Fischer was "incredibly eccentric, possessing strange religious attachments, having a very colorful private life, can be both incredibly rude and charming, unpredictable." Whether Fischer is schizophrenic or not, I do not know.

The point that I am making is that some autistic savants, schizophrenics and epileptics have been the source of great inventions, great feats of the mind. After my vision, I realized that these people were Spirit or Soul Dominant and capable of tapping into a spiritual dimension to come up with ideas that Mind Dominant people are unable, for the most part, to access. Some Spirit or Soul Dominant geniuses have found living as a human being a tremendous struggle.

Obsessive Compulsive Disorder

To be perfectly honest here, I do not know very much about Obsessive Compulsive Disorder (OCD), but my vision managed to put into context some of my childhood OCD behaviors. When I was little, I had to consciously break some very unproductive habits. If I put a glass of water on my nightstand before bed, I would put the cup down and pick it up again and put it down again. In my mind, I had to put the cup down in a particular energy pattern, knowing that with every action, there is an equal and opposite reaction. I intuitively knew that if I did not put the cup down in a particular pattern to create the perfect energy, then something bad might happen to me or to a family member. I hid this compulsion from my parents and siblings, but it used to torment me.

I would hang up my school uniform in my cupboard, not right, do it again, do it again, do it again, until finally in fear, I would stop and get into bed, waiting for something bad to happen. This terrible compulsion permeated many of my activities and it was a tremendous source of anxiety. I finally taught myself to stop by simply telling myself – ENOUGH! Then for the next few days, I would wait for something bad to happen and nothing ever did, so over a short period of time I managed to break this unproductive habit. I am not saying that my method will work for people afflicted with an extreme case of OCD, but I do believe that there may be a connection between OCD and Spirit Dominance.

As a child, I knew that every action created energy. My fear was that I did not know which actions would create a negative outcome, so I would obsess on doing actions over and over again. As I grew older and seriously studied how the human spirit and soul function, I found out that my innate recognition of energy patterns was not so illogical. By way of two stories, I will show what I mean.

About twelve years ago, the city was digging holes in my neighborhood to replace the sewer pipes. I thought this was a great opportunity to gather some rocks to build a retainer wall in my garden. My children and I picked through the dirt and piled stones on our wagon. A neighbor joined us, deciding that she could use some rocks, too, for her landscaping.

A few days later, while I was out for a walk with my children, I saw that same neighbor putting her rocks in her front flower bed. The way she was displaying them made me think of tombstones. I wanted to say to her, "You better not put those rocks like that or someone in your house will die," but I did not know her very well and thought she may think this idea was ludicrous. But, I just knew that she was creating a death energy pattern at the front of her house. Within months, she died of hepatitis.

Another time, I was introduced to a teacher who spent six months of the year in northern Canada with elders in the Native community. She told me that she was weaving the stories of the grandmothers into a book. A sudden thought struck me… she had better not write that book, or she would die of a woman disease. Having gone through my neighbor's death, I became more assertive this time, asking many questions like, "Have you been given permission to write this book by the elders?" "Are you sure it is your purpose to write this book?" "My feeling is that you should not write this book." I never told her that she might die of a woman disease if she wrote this book. I saw her at a luncheon the following June. She was wearing a turban and she told me that she had been through cancer treatment for ovarian cancer, the woman disease.

How does this connect with Obsessive Compulsive Disorder? I have come to understand that some Spirit Dominant people have an unconscious knowledge of the energy patterns of the spiritual dimension. They recognize that they must follow the proper energy patterns to fulfill their desires and their purpose. If they do not, things will not turn out as they planned.

About the time that I had this vision of the Body, Mind, Spirit, Soul Dominance Theory, my son, who had the conversation with God, began to develop the characteristics of OCD. He was exhausted, pale and anxious. I asked him what was wrong. He revealed that he was so worried that I was going to die that he was trying to prevent it by doing the same things over and over. He said that on the way home from school, if he saw a sticker glued on a sign, he would have to jump up and touch it. Back up and touch it, not right, touch it, not right, touch it, not right, touch it. Over and over until finally his friends would drag him away. He believed that if he did not touch it in a certain way that something terrible would happen to me. If it were not the sticker on a sign, it would be a crack on the sidewalk, or setting his alarm clock in the perfect way.

One evening, I had driven out to pick up my older son at his friend's house, leaving my twelve-year-old daughter in charge of babysitting Alex for forty-five minutes. On the way over, a major intersection was shut down because of a fatal accident. There were fire trucks, police cars and ambulances converged, lights still whirling. I was detoured around to the back side of my destination. I stayed a bit too long, talking to the parents of my son's friends and by the time I got home, Alex was in an absolute panic. He had run over to our neighbor's house and insisted they drive to a busy intersection. He told me, "Mom, I didn't know where you were, so I got inside your body and looked out through your eyes. I could see fire trucks, ambulances and police cars. I knew something terrible had happened to you." I told him that indeed he was correct. I did see those things, but that he needed to learn to continue the vision. "Look down. Could you see my arms and legs? If so, then I was not involved in the crash." I wanted to encourage his ability to let his spirit run an errand for him, but wanted to teach him how to grasp the truth.

I do not think that Alex's conversation with God, his ability to take his spirit out of his body to look out through my eyes, his capacity to withstand the pain from his own injuries following a car accident and his obsessive compulsive tendencies are coincidental. I had those tendencies, too. My other two children did not.

I was giving a presentation to a group of teen-agers recently, who were exploring their spiritual capabilities, when one young man asked, "Do you know anything about obsessive compulsive disorders?" I nodded. I believe there is a link between OCD and being Spirit Dominant.

Attention Deficit Disorder

ADD is a term used to describe a person who has difficulty with sustained concentration on a particular task. Often they have short attention spans and begin many projects but leave them unfinished because they cannot maintain their attention long enough. These 'hyper' children pose a problem for parents and teachers because they do not always want to follow along with what everyone else is doing. They interrupt conversations with whatever 'random' idea may strike their imagination.

My vision revealed that these people are actually more sensitive to the energy of the spiritual dimension. They do not often realize that this is what they are doing. They pick up random vibrations and translate the energy into an idea. Maintaining concentration is difficult for them because not only are they trying to focus through the noisy human environment, but they are also trying to tune out the vibrations of the spiritual dimension. Just as thoughts like "You shouldn't put those rocks like that or someone in your house will die," may seem random to my neighbor, illogical and perhaps even crazy, people who have 'ADD' walk through life being inundated with ideas that may seem off-the-wall by Mind/Dominant parents or teachers.

According to my vision, people who are overly sensitive to the spiritual environment must learn how to discern between the human and spiritual plane. They need to learn how to turn the messages that they receive from the spiritual dimension into something practical and meaningful. I suggest that they keep a journal with them at all times and put in it the ideas that just come to them out of the blue. I bet there is a much more logical pattern to these ideas than what could be observed by looking at each idea, one at a time. I would hope that these people would not have their remarkable abilities medicated out of them by chemicals designed to make them more docile and manageable by parents and teachers.

Clinical Depression

The other interesting revelation was that the human spirit craves to be in a place of unconditional love and joy, a place that is like the spiritual dimension we often think of as heaven, the place that I went to in my second near-death experience. If a human being's spirit does not like how the body and mind are being treated, then it may decide to leave the body. Since the spirit is an independent agent, since it is the intangible version of the body and mind, it can leave at will. The spirit can get stuck on people; it can get stuck on a place or even in a time period. Since the first part of the vision said that the spirit can split apart, then that means that the spirit that is living inside of us must be able to split. That means a fraction of the spirit can go to another time and place, leaving our body and mind behind. The person is left to function with only the body and mind and a fraction of the spirit. This can be very lonely and dark. The vision told me that this condition is clinical depression.

Overall Implications

SIDS, autism, schizophrenia, clinical depression, obsessive compulsive disorder and attention deficit disorders are actually spiritual disorders and require a new form of treatment. Those suffering from an inability to take on the human form in a constructive way must be taught how to become human. They must be taught how to thrive in a human body and to enjoy the human experience. Some mind/body people are embarking on adventures to become more spirit and soul. Some Spirit and Soul Dominant people need to learn how to become mind and body. They need to learn that being able to take on the human form is an opportunity that can be very enjoyable.

CONCLUSION

CHAPTER SIXTEEN

An Evolved Human Being

Living is
a thing you do
now or never —
which do you? [56]

Piet Hein (1905 -1996)

ॐ

When I first came up with the Body, Mind, Spirit, Soul Dominance Theory, I started telling anyone who would listen. I have extremely open-minded high school students and some of them have read parts of this book in an attempt to poke holes in it and test its limitations.

Students very often share their spiritual experiences with me. Some reveal that they have seen a ghost in their bedroom, or heard footsteps in the night. Some had been sick when they were younger and remember being on the ceiling looking down. Some have had premonitions. These students said that they were not necessarily Spirit Dominant because they loved the human experience, sports, make-up, hair and such. They had maybe one or two spiritual experiences, or knew someone who had them and were open to the existence of a spiritual dimension. Many students expressed a sense of relief to share their stories, revealing that they thought they were going out of their minds. Most did not share their insights with their parents. Although some of these students are body/mind, they could feel that there was more to life than the material.

What makes these students Body/Mind Dominant and not Spirit Dominant? They use their bodies for sports. They notice the fine details of the world around them. They are visible. The Mind Dominant students engage in class activities, thriving on intellectual challenge. The Spirit Dominant students are often in my non-academic classes, or are coded special education. They very often do not thrive in the current education model, which focuses on body and mind development, not spirit, or soul. There can be Spirit or Soul Dominant children failing in religious schools too, because a religious school does not necessarily nurture individual spirit, but instead may force a student to follow a particular doctrine that is in opposition to what the individual spirit intuitively and experientially knows to be true. I believe that our present school system is failing the Spirit and Soul Dominant child.

I was really excited to see students have such a profound "ah-ha" moment. From a personal perspective, I realized that since I am a Soul Dominant person with a highly developed Spirit Aspect, I tend to daydream a lot and put off physical tasks as long as I can. As soon as I had this vision, I started jogging to ensure that I was strengthening my body. I renovated my house because I finally noticed that none of my kitchen cupboards or drawers would close and that my appliances were all falling apart. I started to get my hair cut every six weeks and now I even have it highlighted. Although I always kept myself in fairly good condition, I noticed that I barely paid attention to the physical aspect of myself. My Masters Degree has now been completed in order to fulfill my Mind Aspect.

The spirit that lives inside each and every one of us can access knowledge, heal the body, influence other human beings and provide an enormous comfort. For many people, however, they have not been taught how to develop their Spirit or Soul Aspect and may have been taught in school to ignore this part of themselves or to view any spiritual understandings as just some figment of their imagination. For many people, their Spirit Aspect has atrophied, shriveled and become imbedded in the unconscious.

The Body, Mind, Spirit, Soul Dominance Theory is the result of a Masters Degree level course called *Philosophy of Mind*. This was a homework exercise. When I arrived in class, excited about the new theory, I felt like I was sixteen years old again, believing that everyone sent their consciousness to another realm and pulled down a truth. Instead, each classmate outlined the many readings he or she had conducted over the week. They wove the great big thinkers together to come up with a framework for the body, mind and spirit relationship.

Reading other thinkers' ideas had never occurred to me. Why would I want to do that? I wanted something new, unique, a theory that we could all use today to improve our lives as individuals, as parents, as employees or leaders, as friends, as daughters and sons and as spouses. And the new theory, which I call the Body, Mind, Spirit, Soul Dominance Theory does just that. My classmates had designed their interpretations of the body, mind, spirit connection by relying on their Mind aspect and what I had done was use my Spirit Aspect. Because of that, I managed to arrive at a brand new theory on human behavior.

The vision confirmed for me that the human being does have a Body, a Mind, a Spirit, a Soul, and a God Aspect, each with distinct capabilities. As we experience the many years of our life on Earth, we can set a goal to fully develop all five aspects of our being.

The Body, Mind, Spirit, Soul Dominance Theory calls into question, "What is an evolved human being?" A Body/Mind Dominant individual may reply: "To become more patient, more generous, more able to love unconditionally". As a Soul Dominant person, I have already developed the aspect that understands my intimate connection to the Oneness of others, my purpose as a teacher and the longing of all human beings for unconditional love. I need to learn how to plan my financial future better, how to keep on top of incoming emails and voicemails, how to take more enjoyment in selecting clothes, or decorating my home and how to cook more aesthetically pleasing meals. Basically, I need to learn how to enjoy the human experience more.

As an adult, and especially after my vision of the Body, Mind, Spirit, Soul Dominance Theory, I realize that there is exquisiteness about being a human being. A fascinating read is Vicki Mackenzie's account of Tenzin Palmo in *Cave in the Snow: A Western Woman's Quest for Enlightenment*.[57] Palmo is an English woman who spent twelve years meditating in a cave 13,000 feet up in the Himalayas. Palmo was certain that male enlightenment and female enlightenment must be different. She decided to isolate herself in a cave so that she could face her true self, her body, mind and spirit. Palmo emerged from the cave with enormous unconditional love for all beings. I admire Palmo's devotion to her spiritual quest and I find her insights invaluable. However, after I finished reading about her quest, I realized that I want to find a way to live a blissful life, one filled with the unconditional love I experienced during my encounter with near-death, while faced with the numerous conflicts of a single day. I want to feel blissful while driving through the center of town during rush hour. I want to feel unconditional love while dealing with a child engaged in a full blown, power struggle temper tantrum. I want to become more enlightened by confronting modern day life, rather than retreating from it.

After this epiphany, I started jogging so that I could get my body physically active and concentrate on breathing more deeply and regularly. I collect recipes now and experiment in the kitchen rather than ripping off lettuce leaves and eating them as if it were a salad. In the past, I would notice that a whole day would go by and I had not eaten. My spirit had eaten and so I thought that my body had. Now I take more pleasure in feeding my body healthy, delectable foods. My daughter and I sometimes go off to the mall just to try on clothes without my charge card, just to get a feel for what looks good on us. These are just some of my efforts to learn how to be a more engaged human being. My present goal is to enlighten my Body Aspect.

When I am dealing with students who would rather retreat into their cozy, dreamy spirit world rather than deal with homework and tests, I find that a conversation in which they are encouraged to describe their interior world works best. The trick is for parents and teachers to provide resources for children to turn their interior worlds into their human, physical worlds. The real trick is to know to ask the question, "Where do you go?" And, most importantly is the patience and enlightenment that comes from really listening, with unconditional love, to the response.

For children who are afraid of the goblins living under their bed, ask them questions about who these goblins are. Ask with interest, as if these experiences are commonplace. Try to normalize their experiences. If a child has an imaginary friend, inquire about the friend's name and what the friend looks like. Ask your child what they talk about together. Do not be too nosy in the process, but be interested without being intrusive. What it comes down to is honoring your child's experience.

I have found, as a high school teacher, that many of my students who are having a difficult time taking on the human form succumb to drugs, alcohol and excessive sleep. These allow for them to escape the realities of life. They do not know why sports, or schoolwork, or mastery of any skill seems more difficult to them than to others. They see the people around them happy and thriving in their life, with many friends and successes. But here they are sinking further and further into a hazy, sublime life. Parents are frustrated, as are teachers. Parents worry about how they will take care of themselves when they are expected to fly from the nest.

What I now know is that these children are very often suffering a spiritual trauma and do not even know it. They have not had their spiritual aspect nurtured and have not been taught how to take on the human form. When I pull my chair up next to these students and ask if I should mark them present or absent on my attendance list, they invariably say that they are here. But when I look into their eyes with a knowing look and say, "Your body is here, but your real you isn't," a sparkle comes into their eyes as if they have been found out at last. We laugh together because they know that I know from first hand experience that we can be in two places at once, that there is a 'real us' and a 'body us'.

Together we spend time talking about their interior world and the 'real' them. As their teacher and mentor, I try my very best to honor the 'real' them and to remind them from time to time to 'remember who they are', especially when they want to resort to drugs and alcohol. Think about alcohol for a minute. Why is it called 'spirit', wine and spirits? Because alcohol simulates the spirit; it makes a person feel, for however temporary, that they have a spirit. The drug of choice for adolescent raves is 'ecstasy', which is a spiritual term that refers to peak experience. Even the drug and alcohol marketers have figured out that if they can connect their harmful substances to spirit, they can make a sale. When my students are engaging in these toxic substances, I ask them to remember who they are. It is amazing how quickly my students want to fight for who they 'really' are and not for the mask they have worn for many years.

There are plenty of books on the market, which urge people for the sake of their health to become more spiritually aware. I have my own ideas on this subject, but will save the techniques that I use for another book. For now, I want to stress that some people are born Spirit Dominant and have a difficult time taking on the human form. Sometimes this happens only on occasion, when life seems just too unbearable, especially if tragedy strikes. This book serves to recognize this truth and to provide suggestions about how to recognize and relate better to a Spirit Dominant person and to provide possibilities for a Spirit Dominant person to find more joy in life. I toyed with the idea of calling these individuals spiritually gifted, but sometimes the insights do not feel like a gift. And our society does not advocate for teaching or mentoring the Spirit Aspect of human beings. I know that religious traditions have been in place for thousands of years and they have their place in spiritual education. But, do they go far enough into teaching humans how to deal with ghosts, out of body experiences, near deaths, complete 'knowings', or the disillusioned spirit, or soul?

Most people have been taught to ignore the longings of their Spirit Aspect and instead concentrate on developing their physical, material and intellectual selves. I have taught several of my Mind and Body Dominant friends how to develop their Spirit Aspect and they are now having spiritual experiences at will. It is possible.

Everybody has a Soul Aspect, a purpose, whether they know it or not. Recognizing that everything that happens to us, good or bad, has a purpose for our personal human development can pull us out of some of our darkest times. Each aspect of ourselves - the Body, Mind, Spirit, Soul and God contributes to our ability to survive. Our Body can fight off danger; our Mind can determine a course of action; our Spirit connects with the spiritual dimension in ways that the body and mind cannot and as a result can assist us during traumatic times. Our Soul Aspect gives meaning to our lives, a reason for staying in the human form even when times are tough, even when the Spirit Aspect would much rather ram a car into a tree, or plunge a butcher knife into the chest. If we can tap into our Soul Aspect during these times of grief, we can ride out the chaotic times knowing that there is a purpose and meaning even if it is unobservable at the time of crisis.

Many years ago, I had a student who was struggling with his homosexuality. His stepfather would not tolerate this boy's identity and made him sleep in a basement room, away from the rest of the family and called him terribly derogatory names. This student stayed after class for a pep talk on several occasions. When he told me what his stepfather was yelling at him, I simply asked, "Are you those things?"

"No," he replied. "Then make a list of who you really are," I told him, "and whenever you doubt, bring out your list and remind yourself. This situation is only temporary with your stepfather. In six months, you will turn eighteen, graduate and move out. Keep your marks up so that you have a chance at a scholarship and don't let your stepfather's anger allow you to lose your own way."

One of the key survival tools that I share with my students is that the purpose to any given traumatic situation will likely not be readily apparent at the time. Only years later, will the true meaning show itself. At that time, we can use the traumatic experience as a way of assisting others in coping with their own crises. At that time, we will find more meaning and value in the trauma and recognize it as part of our soul purpose.

About three years ago, I saw this same student once again in a restaurant and he came over and gave me a huge hug. He said that he had posted the list about who he 'really' was on the wall of his bedroom and it got him through the toughest times. After graduation, he had moved to Vancouver and worked several years to earn enough money for university and he was entering Teacher's College in the fall. He wanted to pass on the message to other young people – to remember who they are.

This particular student needed to explore all aspects of who he really was, not the masks, but the 'real' him, his Spirit. By exploring and reinforcing the qualities of his Spirit self, he managed to expand that aspect. In doing so, he discovered his Soul's purpose and became more insightful about discrimination. By working on his Spirit and Soul Aspects, he was able to overcome an extremely difficult family situation, one that could have broken him.

A couple of years after my Mom died, my father had a profound sense that he did not have a purpose in life any more. He was always one of my greatest mentors because I remember him telling me when I was a child, "When you choose a career, choose one that serves your country, your society, not just you. Don't choose a career just for the money. Choose one that has meaning." Although I knew that I was to be a teacher by that point in my life, I still took to heart what he said. I can see now that my father led a very purpose driven life. His adult years were about his work in the Department of National Defense and his family. He was always taking care of people, whether it was the citizens of Canada during the Cold War, or his children when they would get a flat tire on their bicycles. My dad retired about the same time his children all moved out of Ottawa and started families of their own. But when the love of his life, my mother, died, he felt very alone and purposeless. He no longer had anyone to take care of.

We were talking about his purpose, or perceived lack thereof, when I finally looked at him and said, "By the end of today, you will know your purpose." Because I have spent years developing my Spirit Aspect, I have come to realize that if we want to know something, we simply need to ask. My father asked me about his purpose that day and I sent his question into the spirit dimension. By putting a specific time limit on the response - in this case it was the end of the day - we were able to recognize the response when it came.

Within a few hours of me sending my Dad's request to the spirit dimension, the telephone rang. It turned out that it was the husband of a patient who had died at the local hospital about six months earlier. My father volunteers one night a week in the Intensive Care Unit waiting room of the hospital. Six months prior, a man had lost the love of his life after nearly fifty years of marriage. My father had given him his calling card and told him that if ever life became unbearable, that it did not seem worth living any more, to give him a call.

The same day I told my Dad that he would soon learn his purpose, he began to expand his notion of what his purpose was. My father was left behind for a reason. He needed to learn to use his heartache to help others. He soon realized that maybe he needed to reach out to other widowed men, because he knew exactly how it felt to lose the love of his life.

My point is that ever since this vision came to me, I have learned that we all have a purpose in life. In many cases it is this purpose that pulls us out of dark times. I have also learned that if we ask for our purpose, we will most likely receive an answer instantaneously if we are aware enough to make the connection.

At the time of this writing, I have a sixteen-year-old student who is living on his own. He intervened on behalf of his mother who was being beaten by his father. He was kicked out for defying his father. For months, he went from friend to friend, sleeping on couches and trying to muster up enough energy to make his way to school. One day, I caught a glimpse of cut marks on his arms beneath his long sleeve black shirt. I pulled my chair up for a discussion. This boy continued to have bright, cheerful eyes, even in his darkest times. The cutting was a sign that he had finally reached his breaking point. We talked about this point in his life being temporary and that some day he would discover the significance of this tragedy and use it as part of his soul's purpose. He had to stay anchored in his soul purpose – that he is a meaningful, significant human being who was sent to Earth with a purpose. His task was to seek out that purpose.

This student spent one semester in my English class and I encouraged him to write about his experiences. He did not write about the darkness; he wrote about adventure and magic. One memorable story was called *Hero Ant*. He loved writing about the little seemingly insignificant beings making something of themselves. He signed up for another one of my classes because he said that he needed to stay with me to feel anchored, to stay focused on the idea that someday he would survive the trauma of being rejected by his family. His purpose or Soul Aspect is keeping him focused and alive. At the moment, he is writing a series of children's stories, all with the focus of how little children, who are facing unspeakable circumstances, can draw upon the hero (or soul) within to conquer dark times.

Since I am divorced, my children spend one week-end with me and the other with their Dad. At first, I felt very lost. I was heartbroken that I could not see my children every single morning, that I would not be a part of their lives every day. Soon I realized that I was wasting a lot of valuable time feeling sorry for myself. It was not going to change my circumstances. The moment they left for their Dad's, I gave myself five minutes to feel sorry for myself and then I spent the rest of the week-end exploring the 'real' me, my desires and my purpose, my Spirit and my Soul.

Now when I come home from work on Friday afternoon, I jump on my couch and tell the universe, The Force of Oneness, or God, that I am available to be used as a tool to fulfill other avenues of my ultimate purpose, my reason for being, which goes beyond being a high school English teacher. Remember in John F. Kennedy's famous speech, he said, "Ask not what your country can do for you, but what you can do for your country." I take these Friday afternoons, or entire week-ends to say, "Ask not what the Force of Oneness or God can do for me, but what I can do for God." My days are filled with magical moments that only can come from being open to force of the universe.

For example, one weekend I announced my availability and the next thing I knew I felt like dashing out to the store to buy some pretty note cards. This was a rather spontaneous and random effort on my part, or so it seemed at first. Once I arrived home, I made a pot of herbal tea and got out my address book. I went all the way from A-Z in my book writing letters. The funny thing is that at first I was going to write everyone I knew, but before long I noticed that I was writing a letter to my Mom's brother and sister-in-law, my Mom's dear friend, my Mom's nieces, my sisters and brother, and so it went. I was compelled to tell each one that I loved them and missed them and that we should always stay connected. I truly feel that I had made myself available to my mother that afternoon so that she could connect up from the spiritual dimension to her loved ones who remain here on Earth.

Another week-end, I made myself available and the next thing I knew, my neighbor was asking if I could meet with her aunt-in-law who was becoming severely depressed because her husband announced that he did not love her anymore. After thirty years of marriage and two or three children, he wanted a divorce. He gave her two weeks to move out. I met with this dear, fragile woman and the next thing I knew she had fire in her eyes and had come to realize that she was much stronger than she thought. She was clearly more optimistic and ready to start a new life.

When I returned from coffee with this woman, there was a call on my answering machine from a friend who had lost his wife to cancer eight years ago. He is a family friend and he bought a house four blocks from me. He had finally sold the old furniture and had started completely new with all leather couches and a new dining room suite. We had a celebratory glass of wine and I could see how he had started a new chapter of his life.

I returned from this visit to check my emails and there were two, one from a woman that I met at a conference who had decided to quit her teaching job and start practicing law once again. She wrote that she was afraid of starting something new, but excited at the same time. The other email was from a photographer friend of mine. We wanted to do a project together focused on overcoming the woes of divorce. Our goal was to create a workshop for people who wanted to stay true to themselves in the midst of a chaotic and sometimes mean-spirited divorce. Since my weekend directed me to all sorts of people who were struggling with new beginnings, not just divorce, we decided to widen our focus to those who are in the throes of transforming any facet of their lives.

I find that when I leave myself open for the God Force of Oneness to use me as a tool, the most remarkable things happen. If I look back, I can see the pattern to the tasks that I am given and this reveals to me what my purpose is. I do recommend that you start each day off with a connection to your Soul and God Aspects, to open yourself up while you are going about your day for the many possibilities of being a valuable tool. I also recommend that you clear your calendar for a day, or week-end, or even longer and become open to the universe, become available. You will most certainly feel the magic of what will come.

I happened to learn my purpose early in life. Only lately has my purpose, to be a teacher, begun to evolve. I am now coming to realize that I need to broaden my perception of the word – teacher. By making myself available to the universe, my notion of being a teacher evolves. It expands and grows. We all need to think of our purpose in an expanded way, not in just a singular, narrow definition.

I have been teaching high school English for nearly twenty-three years and I love it. I find though that students continue to tell me that I have a radical way of teaching English because they learn more about themselves than they do the characters in the story. My method of teaching is to encourage self-reflection, to permit students to examine why they do the things they do by comparing themselves to the characters that they study. We ponder, theorize, adjust our thinking, challenge each other and, ultimately, realize that we are all evolving human beings.

We reflect on the literature through the lens of various religious belief systems of the members of the class. For example, how would a Muslim family react to Romeo and Juliet running off and getting married without parental permission. And according to Muslim faith, what would happen to Romeo and Juliet after they committed suicide? Would they go to heaven or hell, or is there such a place? What about a Buddhist interpretation, or Christian, or Hindu?

In my classroom, students are given the opportunity to share their personal experiences with spirit. The spirit dimension is not a taboo subject. When the witches appear in Shakespeare's *Macbeth*, I ask if anyone has ever been to a fortuneteller. We talk about whether any of the predictions came true. We explore Macbeth's reaction to the witches' prediction that he will become king some day. When the ghosts appear in *Macbeth* and *Hamlet*, I ask if anyone has ever seen a ghost. Most students in the class have a ghost story to tell, either from personal experience, or from a friend or family member. Some students believe a ghost lives in their house and are eager to share their stories. Though I was taught in high school that only uneducated people believe in spiritual phenomenon, I encourage tolerance in the classroom so that everyone feels safe to share their reality without ridicule.

Invariably when lunch break occurs, a knock will come at my classroom door. One or two students will venture in to share their most intimate experiences with spirit. They are shy at first, claiming that this is the first time that they have ever openly talked about ghosts, visions and dreams. Some thought that they were going crazy, but when I openly say that I have seen a ghost, they suddenly felt as though they were not crazy after all. Because I have always been open about my encounters, I cannot help but be surprised that others keep theirs' locked up within. To me, these types of experiences are so normal, so a part of my every day life that I really do not think twice about telling someone of a vision just as I would pass along the weather report.

My purpose – to be a teacher – has evolved to teaching others that we can share our spiritual experiences, understandings and insights. Students have demonstrated a desire to honor their purpose in life, as shown in their Seven Wonders list that I mentioned earlier. Therefore, we talk about the concept of purpose in life and whether that is an important consideration for selecting a career. Many of my adolescent students struggle with their identity. They feel that they wear several masks to please their parents, teachers and friends. They hope that once they are adults that they can shed these masks and become the 'real' them, which they describe as their spirit. They hope to connect with their soul, which they feel is waiting for them in the afterlife.

I agree with many of my students who view the soul as something more distant from the body, mind and spirit. As much as I believe that we can be Soul Dominant, I also believe that there is a droplet of soul within us and the bulk of our soul is in the spirit dimension, waiting for us on the sidelines according to my metaphor of the soul coach who sends our spirit into the game of life. The soul droplet anchors us to the spirit dimension and when we die we will be reconnected to the rest of our soul.

The traditional circle of life typically includes birth, aging and death. As an alternative, think of it in terms of Body, Mind, Spirit, Soul and God development. Wherever you start in terms of the five aspects on your unique human evolution, whether it is Body Dominant, Mind Dominant, Spirit Dominant, Soul Dominant, try to fully develop your next strongest aspect, then the next, and so on, until you feel that you have expanded all aspects of yourself. Many people believe that becoming more spiritual is part of life's purpose and it probably is. But for a Spirit Dominant person, who longs for the tranquility and unconditional love of the spirit dimension and who, as a result, retreats into sleep for comfort or has difficulty staying in relationships, she might think about coming to terms with her Body Aspect.

Recently, my friend helped me repair the downspouts of my eaves troughs, as a rather large puddle of water was accumulating on my basement floor during a prolonged rainstorm. As nice as he was, I could see in his expression that he was rather surprised that I would let this problem go untreated for such a long time. I would way rather sit at my computer day after day writing this book than fix the downspout. I consider learning how to manage my money and understanding investment strategies as becoming a better human being. These days my eyes glaze over when I have to deal with discussion around financial planning. I would rather let the universe provide, but at some point I do have to perform the human tasks of organizing my money, as painful as that is for me. I also want to enjoy more of the sensuous parts of being a human being, like cooking a variety of delicious foods, playing sports, jogging on a regular basis and paying attention to my physical appearance.

Significance of the Dominance Theory

This new theory that was conveyed to me in a vision has significant ramifications. In terms of our educational system and our understanding of how to parent our children, we must realize that not all children relate to their body, mind, spirit and soul in the same way. Our community has a wide array of sporting events from hockey to gymnastics, to martial arts, to soccer. Shopping malls display the latest fashions. Street corners host numerous beauty salons. Children in North America must attend school until they are sixteen years old. Again their Body Aspect is supported in the curriculum through physical education classes, extracurricular sports, fashion and foods classes. Their Mind Aspect is developed through math, science, social studies and English classes, along with accounting, computer applications, and more.

How is the Spirit Aspect of our children nurtured? Do teachers and parents recognize that some children are not as physical as others and may instead rest in a perennial numbed out state of the 'daydream' or spirit world? Do parents realize that their children are trying to stay in their spirit state, the state that feels the most natural and comfortable to them? Do parents and teachers recognize that some children need to learn how to move along the circle of development and learn how to be human? Most people think that being human is normal. It is not normal for a number of our children. They need to be taught, not forced, but taught that there is an exquisiteness to being a human being, that there is a very pleasurable aspect to it. As Piet Hien encourages in his poem at the start of this chapter, *living is a thing you do – now or never, which do you?* He poses an essential 'meaning of life' question. When I learned about the Dominance Theory in my vision, I learned that I needed to take the act of living more seriously. And parents, as well as teachers, need to understand how to encourage children to make their exterior, tangible, physical, human existence match their magical, peaceful and creative interior world of spirit.

Physicians need to recognize the difference between a physical, mental, or spiritual ailment. These three aspects work interdependently. Therefore, the physician must determine how to incorporate the Spirit Aspect into the treatment plan of a patient. When the body goes into trauma, perhaps through a near-death experience, the physician must learn how to continue contact with the spirit while working on the body. Many who have gone through a near-death experience have regained earthly consciousness revealing similar stories. Many of them recall hearing their name called and it was at that moment that they returned to their body. This happened to me during my near-death experience as well. Are surgeons aware that by calling the patient by name, there is a greater chance the spirit will stay in the body, which in turn would increase the success rate of any particular surgeon?

Countless studies have demonstrated that prayer increases patient wellness. As a result, medicine is currently integrating a spiritual component to the treatment package of patients. However, the idea that a patient has a spirit and that this spirit must be understood as intricately as the functioning of the heart, lungs and circulatory system, is still a radical idea for most doctors.

For mental health practitioners, the Dominance Theory is a brand new way of examining patients who have difficulty with daily life. Spirit Dominant children can be deeply misunderstood in our school system. I would like to take on, as part of my life's mission, the task of advocating for these Spirit Dominant students. I would like to design a strategy for teachers to recognize these children and get them the appropriate mentor so that their true genius can emerge.

The time has come to accept the fact that the human being has a spirit and a soul. It is not just a philosophical matter any more. Too many people are having spiritual encounters and yet few have a way of processing them in our North American society. Neuroscientists have discovered a 'God Spot' in the brain and Dean Hamer has found a genetic explanation for Spirit and Soul Dominant individuals. We cannot ignore that the Spirit and Soul Aspects of the human being is in all facets of our lives from education to medicine, from parenting to befriending. The time has come to address the Spirit and Soul. We cannot ignore it any longer.

The Last Question

So far, I have presented the vision that I had that answered the question, *"What is the relationship between body, mind, spirit?"* I kept to the exact understandings as perceived on that Friday afternoon four years ago. Just as I was finishing off this piece, I posed one last question, "What else do I need to know?" Again, I got an answer and it surprised me yet again. It said, "You barely colored in your Soul Aspect. You have studied the body, mind and spirit. Now you will learn more about the human soul. Your Soul Aspect is about to expand and with that – your purpose."

Am I ever excited! I knew, when I embarked on the quest of organizing the theory for presentation, that until I finished, I would not receive any more insights into my own spiritual development. I am deeply honored that I have now been deemed ready to gain insight into my Soul Aspect.

References

INTRODUCTION

[1] Coelho, P. (1998). *The Alchemist*. San Francisco: HarperCollins. (p.166).
[2] Ibid. (p.24).

CHAPTER ONE

[3] Wyndham, J. (1958). *The Chrysalids*. London: Penguin Books. (p. 5).
[4] Ibid. (p. 5).

CHAPTER TWO

[5] Steinbeck, J. (1992). *The Grapes of Wrath*. New York: Penguin Books. (p. 26).
[6] Ibid. (p. 439).

CHAPTER THREE

[7] Anderson, L. (1999). *Speak*. New York: Penguin Books. (p. 10).
[8] Myss, C. (2003). *Sacred contracts: Awakening our divine potential*. New York: Three Rivers Press.
[9] Lewis, T. (2002). *Seven Wonders*. In R. Davies, G. Kirkland, & J. Siamon (Eds.), *Crossroads* (pp. 246-251). Toronto: Gage Learning Corporation

CHAPTER FOUR

[10] Shakespeare, W. (1997). *Hamlet*. Toronto: International Thomson Publishing. Act I, Sc.v.ll 184-185.

CHAPTER FIVE

[11] Lewis, T. (2002). *Seven Wonders*. In R. Davies, G. Kirkland, & J. Siamon (Eds.), *Crossroads* (pp. 246-251). Toronto: Gage Learning Corporation.

CHAPTER SIX

[12] Albom, M. (1997). *tuesdays with Morrie*. New York: Random House. (p. 119).

CHAPTER SEVEN

[13] Brooke, R. (1983). *The Hill*. In S. Paustian (Ed). *Through the open window*. Toronto: Oxford University Press

CHAPTER EIGHT

[14] Crowfoot. (1983). *Farewell.* In S. Paustian (Ed.), *Through the open window* (p. 62). Toronto: Oxford University Press.

[15] Godridge, T. (2002). *Your Baby from 6 to 12 months: A Step-by-Step Guide for Parents.* New York: DK Publishing, Inc.

CHAPTER NINE

[16] Hesse, H. (1951). *Siddhartha.* New York: New Directions Publication Corporation. (p. 31).

[17] Gelb, M. (2002). *Discover your genius: How to think like history's ten most revolutionary minds.* New York: HarperCollins. (p. 316).

CHAPTER TEN

[18] Laurence, M. (1981). *Horses of the night.* In T. Ford (Ed.). *Story & structure* (pp.8-24). Toronto: Academic Press Canada.

[19] Hardy, A. (1979). *The spiritual nature of man: A study of contemporary religious experience.* Oxford: Clarence Press.

[20] Hay, D. & Nye, R. (1998). *The Spirit of the Child.* London: Parragon Book Service Limited. Note: I tried to locate a copy of The Spirit of the Child. Unfortunately, I could not find a single copy. It was quoted in numerous publications.

CHAPTER ELEVEN

[21] Dickenson, E. *If I can Stop one heart from breaking.* www.catholic-animals.org

[22] MacDougall, Fraser. (2006). Note: I feel close to my nephew Fraser and so I am putting a plug in here for him because I know how Soul Dominant people can struggle to make a dream come true. Visit Fraser's website at www.frasermacdougall.com

[23] Davies, R. (1970). *Fifth business.* Toronto: Penguin Books. (pp. 196-197).

[24] Pickels, D. (2002). *Joan of Arc.* Philadelphia: Chelsea House Publishers.(p. 52).

[25] Ibid. (p. 52).

[26] Ibid. (pp. 54-55).

[27] Ibid. (p. 171).

[28] Greenberg, J. and Jordan, S. (2001). *Vincent Van Gogh: Portrait of an artist.* New York: Delacorte Press. (p. 25).

[29] Ibid. (p. 20).

[30] Ibid. (p. 76).

[31] Harris, N. (1996). *Masterworks: Van Gogh.* London: Parragon Book Service Limited. (p.41).

[32] Greenberg, J. and Jordan, S. (2001) *Vincent Van Gogh: Portrait of an artist.* New York: Delacorte Press. (p. 99).

[33] Ibid. (p. 103).

[34] Frank, J. (2002). *Dostoevsky: The mantle of the prophet, 1871-1881.* Princeton, New Jersey: Princeton University Press.

[35] Ibid. (p. 30).

[36] Ibid. (p. 246).

CHAPTER TWELVE

[37] Frank, A. (1991). From the diary of a young girl. In D. Saliani (Ed.). *Poetry Alive* (p.132). Toronto: Copp Clark Pitman Ltd.

CHAPTER THIRTEEN

[38] Hus, A. (1962). *Greek and roman religion.* New York: Hawthorne Books. (p. 148).

[39] Hearnshaw, L.(1987). *The shaping of modern psychology: An historical introduction.* New York:Routledge & Kegan Paul, Inc.

[40] Ibid.

[41] Ibid.

[42] Ibid.

[43] Hearnshaw, L.(1987). *The shaping of modern psychology: An historical introduction.* New York:Routledge & Kegan Paul, Inc. (1991).

[44] Ibid.

CHAPTER FOURTEEN

[45] Perkins, C. (1982). *The Yellow Wallpaper.* In A. Landy & D. Martin (Eds). *The Heath Introduction to Literature* (p. 106). Toronto: D.C. Heath Canada Ltd.

[46] Persinger, M. (1987). http://laurentian.ca/neurosci/_people/Persinger.html

[47] Morse, M. and Perry, P. (2000). *Where God lives: The science of the paranormal and how our brains are linked to the universe.* New York: HarperCollins.

[48] Ramachandran, V.S. and Blakeslee, S. (1998). *Phantoms in the brain: Probing the mysteries of the human mind.* New York: William Morrow and Company, Inc.

[49] Gelb, M. (2002). *Discover your genius: How to think like history's ten most revolutionary minds.* New York: HarperCollins.

[50] Newberg, A. & D'Aquili, E. (2001). *Why God won't go away: Brain science and the biology of belief.* New York: Ballantine Books. http://www.csp.org/chrestomathy/why_god.html

[51] Hamer, D. (2004). *The God gene: How faith is hardwired into our genes.* New York: Doubleday.

[52] Alper, M. (2000). *The "God" part of the brain: A scientific interpretation of human spirituality and God.* New York: Rogue Press.

[53] Bibby, R. (2001). Canada's teen: Today, yesterday, and tomorrow. Toronto: Stoddard Publishing, Co.

CHAPTER FIFTEEN

[54] Blake, W. Infant joy (1991). In D. Saliani, L. Liffiton & J. McAllister (Eds). *Poetry alive: Transitions* (p.11). Toronto: Copp Clark Pitman Ltd.

[55] Nasar, S. (1998). *A beautiful mind: The life of mathematical genius and nobel laureate John Nash.* New York: Simon & Schuster. (p. 11).

[56] Hein, P. (1991). Living is. In D. Saliani (Ed.). *Poetry alive* (p.73). Toronto: Copp Clark Pitman Ltd.

[57] Mackenzie,V. (1998). *Cave in the snow: A western woman's quest for enlightenment.* London: Bloomsbury.

Biography

Margot McKinnon (B.A., B.Ed., M.A.) is a teacher, mother, and public speaker in Calgary, Alberta. Undaunted by the skepticism of society toward spiritual encounters, she courageously advocates for spiritual intelligence as a legitimate 'way of knowing'.

McKinnon may be contacted through email at: mlmckin@telus.net.

AB Reliability Standards

(1) Information Protection

(2) Configuration, Chg. Mgmt,
Vulnerability Assessments

(3) Recovery Plans For BES
Cyber
Systems

Incident Reporting & Response

Syst. Security Mgmt

* Physical Security of BES
Cyber Systems

Electronic Security Parameters

Personnel & Training
Security Mgmt. Controls
BES Cyber System Categorization